A MARGAR

Other Margareader® Books

THE ESSENTIAL BOOK OF BOAT DRINKS
& Assorted Frozen Concoctions
Olaf Nordstom

JIMMY'S BUFFET
Food for Feeding Friends & Feeding Frenzies
Olaf Nordstrom

THE ESSENTIAL BOOK OF TEQUILA
Olaf Nordstom

THE OCCASIONAL MARGAREADER:
Food for Thought Served Buffett Style
Donald W. Davidson

TENTH EDITION

THINGS YOU KNOW by HEART

1001 Questions from the Songs of

Jimmy Buffett

by Olaf Nordstrom

The Peninsula Press

Cape Cod, Nantucket & Martha's Vineyard

Margareader® is a registered trademark of The Peninsula Press

Things You Know by Heart
1001 Questions from the Songs of Jimmy Buffett

is published by
The Peninsula Press · Cape Cod 02670 USA
Donald W. Davidson
Publisher

Additional copies of this and other Margareader® titles may be ordered at
WWW.MARGAREADER.COM

Library of Congress Catalog Card Number: 17-80875
Nordstrom, Olaf.
   Things You Know by Heart: 1001 Questions from the Songs of Jimmy Buffett
   The Peninsula Press, ©2017.
   ISBN: 1-883684-19-6

Tenth Edition
Manufactured in the United States of America
1 2 3 4 5 6 7 8 9 0 / 26 25 24 23 22 21 20 19 18 17

First Look

Nothing remains quite the same

SO, HERE WE ARE. After more than twenty years in print, this little volume opens with yet another new page for the current age. Well, sort of. If you own one or more of the earlier editions of this book, then the next few paragraphs are pretty much déjà, déjà, déjà vu. (If this is your first reading, though, I guess it's vujà dé: the feeling that you've never been here before.)

Whatever your situation, the once and future subtitle of this book – 1001 Questions from the Songs of Jimmy Buffett – remains the very same. And it still reminds me of the words of my grandfather.

"The world can be divided into three kinds of people," he'd often say. "Those who work well with numbers and those who don't." And then he'd pause with a sigh of resignation before admitting the family's shortcomings. "You and I don't."

For more than half a century, in fact, numbers have done nothing more than numb my brain. If I run into a sum with a couple of numbers, I wind up thinking all night.

I'm telling you this because – of all the things that have changed with this 10th edition – the title and subtitle cannot be counted among them. As always, some people will want to blame me just because the correct total of all the questions and answers now far exceeds the number that's always been stated on the cover.

Back when I compiled the original 1001 questions (along with nearly 1000 correct answers!) I had made my own rule that these questions ought to be based only on stuff that Jimmy sings on his recordings. By the 4th edition, though, I had changed my mind a bit, and here's why it's not my fault.

Since this book first came into print, Jimmy's continued to broaden his own horizons, so to speak, and his renown no longer is based upon just a lifetime of recordings, as well as a couple of best-selling books. Not one to sit still or to rest his own imagination, Jimmy has continued to tour, to record, and to write in order to keep us all entertained with those stories that only he can tell.

So, as I had noted in the foreword to that 4th edition some years ago, I decided back then to cast off the shackles of my own restrictions and to add a new category of questions (cleverly) titled "Off the Record" just to deal with all those other, non-recording things that Jimmy had been creating. For that reason, then, there are more than 1001 questions in this book.

While I've been updating all the questions, I've also fine tuned what we believe to be the most accurate and most extensive catalogue of every commercial recording that Jimmy Buffett has ever been associated with. I qualify these as "commercial" recordings in order to distinguish them from live performances, as well as those videos and appearances that were intended only for broadcast. In some cases, Jimmy appears only as a background vocalist; in one or two, as a non-performing writer. For those who enjoy collecting Jimmy's recordings, I hope that this serves you as an invaluable guide. In short, it strives to be the official record of all his recordings.

Now, despite the fact that Jimmy has been working hard and that I've been trying to keep pace with him, the publisher of this book has done absolutely nothing to change the subtitle of this volume. So, if you still have any sort of problem with the fact that all these questions really do add up to more than the 1001 mentioned on the cover, then consider these two possibilities: (a) you're getting more than you thought you were paying for and/or (b) we just might be related.

OLAF NORDSTROM
24.33°N 81.48°W / 1 January 17
Same Spot / Different Day

INDECISIONS / NUMBER 1:

The INDECISIONS form of question may or may not be the easiest throughout this book, but we have to begin somewhere. So, let's get your toes wet.

The thirteen greatest hit(s) collected in the 1985 Lp called Songs You Know by Heart remain not only at the core of Jimmy's repertoire, but also as essential knowledge for any true Parrot Head. Which of the following songs are included on this album?

1. YES/NO: Fins

2. YES/NO: Last Mango in Paris

3. YES/NO: Volcano

4. YES/NO: Grapefruit-Juicy Fruit

5. YES/NO: Changes in Latitudes, Changes in Attitudes

6. YES/NO: The Captain and the Kid

7. YES/NO: Come Monday

8. YES/NO: One Particular Harbour

9. YES/NO: A Pirate Looks at Forty

10. YES/NO: Gypsies in the Palace

Answers are on the next page . . .

ANSWERS:

1.   Fins/YES

2.   Last Mango in Paris/NO

3.   Volcano/YES

4.   Grapefruit-Juicy Fruit/YES

5.   Changes in Latitudes, Changes in Attitudes/YES

6.   The Captain and the Kid/NO

7.   Come Monday/YES

8.   One Particular Harbour/NO

9.   A Pirate Looks at Forty/YES

10.   Gypsies in the Palace/NO

 Things to Know by Chart:

KEY WEST, FLORIDA
Latitude: 28° N
Longitude: 82° W

Don' chu know / number 1:

Okay, now that you've got your feet wet, let's wade in a bit deeper with a Don' chu know set from Songs You Know by Heart.

Correctly match the number of the measurement of time with the letter of the Song You (Should) Know by Heart. To score correctly, you may use a song title only once.

11.	70 days	a.	Come Monday
12.	3 days	b.	Boat Drinks
13.	All season	c.	Changes in Latitudes, Changes in Atttudes
14.	No time	d.	Cheeseburger in Paradise
15.	2 weeks	e.	He Went to Paris
16.	4 days	f.	Pencil Thin Mustache
17.	20 years	g.	A Pirate Looks at Forty
18.	A little while	h.	Margaritaville
19.	A weekend	i.	Grapefruit-Juicy Fruit
20.	Century	j.	Fins
		k.	Volcano
		l.	None

Answers are on the next page . . .

ANSWERS:

11. d: 70 days/Cheeseburger in Paradise

12. j: 3 days/Fins

13. h: All season/Margaritaville

14. k: No time/Volcano

15. g: 2 weeks/A Pirate Looks at Forty

16. a: 4 days/Come Monday

17. e: 20 years/He Went to Paris

18. i: A little while/Grapefruit-Juicy Fruit

19. c: A weekend/Changes in Latitudes, Changes in Attitudes

20. b: Century/Boat Drinks

 Things to Know by Chart:

MOBILE, ALABAMA
Latitude: 30° N
Longitude: 88° W

DIS & DAT / NUMBER 1:

Well, now, you might think that this is getting just a little tougher than you first imagined, but I doubt that you're in over your head. We'll stick with those Songs You Know by Heart just a little while longer until we see whether you're going to sink or swim.

21. So, how DO you like your cheeseburgers cooked?

22. Where did you go for adventure?

23. What were you never meant for?

24. What practice once was limited to jazz musicians?

25. What three things have you seen more than you can recall?

26. What do you want from the barmaid?

27. How much money have you made?

28. If you had a bottle of Green Label rum, what might you be writing in the islands?

29. What are you glad not to live in?

30. Who disrupted your plan to go out for a bite?

Answers are on the next page . . .

ANSWERS:

21. Medium rare/CIP

22. Out on the sea/SOASOAS

23. Glitter rock & roll/CM

24. Smoking marijuana/PTM

25. Good times, riches, and son-of-a-bitches/CIL,CIA

    [Note: In some versions edited for radio airplay, the term "son-of-a-bitches" has been changed to "some scars and stitches." This edit originated when the British Broadcasting Corporation (BBC) did not permit the original lyric to be aired, and that version can sometimes be heard today.]

26. A pitcher, another round/WDWGDAS

27. Enough to buy Miami/APLAF

28. Your memoirs/HWTP

29. A trailer/SOASOAS

30. A chum with a bottle of rhum/CIL,CIA

 Things to Know by Chart:

SEA OF CORTEZ
Latitude: 25° N
Longitude: 110° W

Dis & Dat / Number 2:

Good to see that you've still got your head above water and that you're willing to take a shot at another ten questions. Just to keep you comfortable, we'll stick with just the Songs You Know by Heart for one more page, and then we'll chart a course for open waters.

31. What ultimatum does your girlfriend give as the ground begins to move?

32. What diet is said to raise the dead?

33. What have the newspapers advertised lately?

34. What sort of cake do you nibble on?

35. Where can you see it all there?

36. What are the boys in the band screaming?

37. How much money have you made?

38. What would you do with your honey if you had the money?

39. What are you glad not to live in?

40. Who disrupted your plan to go out for a bite?

Answers are on the next page . . .

ANSWERS:

31. Love me now or love me not/VOL
     [Note: Actually, Jimmy's volcanic pun is: "Lava me now or lava me not."]

32. Warm beer and bread/CIP

33. Cheap airfare/BD

34. Sponge cake/MAR

35. The movies/PTM

36. Boat drinks!/BD

37. Enough to buy Miami/APLAF

38. Strap her in beside you; never leave her alone/GFJF

39. A trailer/SOASOAS

40. A chum with a bottle of rhum/CIL,CIA

Things to Know by Chart:

KINGSTON, JAMAICA
Latitude: 18° N
Longitude: 76° W

DON' CHU KNOW / NUMBER 2:

Correctly match the number of the article of clothing with the letter of the song in which it is mentioned. To score correctly, you may use a song title only once.

41. Ballroom gown   a. Turn Up the Heat and Chill the Rose

42. Uggs   b. Don' Chu Know

43. Blue jeans   c. Why the Things We Do

44. Muu muu   d. In the Shelter

45. Tony Lama boots   e. Miss You So Badly

46. Boots and socks   f. Quietly Making Noise

47. Sequined suit   g. Livingston's Gone to Texas

48. G (string)   h. You Call It Jogging

49. Felt beret   i. Cowboy in the Jungle

50. Barefoot shoes   j. Brand New Country Star

   k. Livingston Saturday Night

   l. None

Answers are on the next page . . .

ANSWERS:

41. l: Ballroom gown/None

42. a: Uggs/Turn Up the Heat and Chill the Rose

43. b: Blue jeans/Don' Chu Know

44. i: Muu muu/Cowboy in the Jungle

45. k: Tony Lama boots/Livingston Saturday Night

46. d: Boots and socks/In the Shelter

47. j: Sequined suit/Brand New Country Star

48. e: G (string)/Miss You So Badly

49. f: Felt beret/Quietly Making Noise

50. c: Barefoot shoes/Why the Things We Do

 Things to Know by Chart:

EVERGLADES, FLORIDA
Latitude: 26° N
Longitude: 80° W

DIS & DAT / NUMBER 3:

51. What kinds of music does the Bob Roberts Society Band not play?

52. What is it that turns the tide from a walk on the beach to the wild side?

53. Who tells everybody what to do in the islands?

54. Who is it that you think owes you a favor?

55. Who had loved Livingston as though he were her husband?

56. Who will glue you to the floor?

57. What did the townsfolk try to kill with their Bibles and their stills?

58. Who dresses like the city girls do?

59. Where was it that stars fell?

60. What kind of drink did the husbands share in Cayo Hueso?

Answers are on the next page . . .

ANSWERS:

51. Grunge and loud/BRSB

52. A howlin' moon/HM

53. Bwana Jim/MN

54. Jesus/CHR

55. Holly/LGTT

56. A lover/LAL

57. Reality/TS

58. Your fast-moving angel/PTSY

59. Alabama/SFOA

60. A Coke/EGACIM

Things to Know by Chart:

CARIBBEAN SEA, WEST INDIES
Latitude: 15° N
Longitude: 78° W

DIS & DAT / NUMBER 4:

61. After watching the The Gong Show, what program do you await?

62. What happens to those who cut classes at Domino College?

63. Why did you take a weekend off last month?

64. What would you do if you had it all to do over again?

65. What would a hard luck hero spend his money on?

66. How does the freezing weather affect your ears?

67. What did Mr. Peabody's train haul away?

68. Where do you go once the anchor is down and the sails are furled?

69. With what do you wash down your Darvon?

70. What do all the days spent together and apart add up to?

Answers are on the next page . . .

ANSWERS:

61. Zorro/MYSB

62. They track you through the jungle and kick your ass/DC

63. To try to recall the whole year/CIL,CIA

64. Get drunk and jump back in/LF

65. Grass/PBC

66. You can't feel them/TAB

67. The town of Paradise/PAR

68. On the road/PB

69. Orange juice/MHH

70. Nothing/SIUTL

 Things to Know by Chart:

MISSOULA, MONTANA
Latitude: 46° N
Longitude: 114° W

Don' chu know / number 3:

Correctly match the number of the musical performer(s) with the letter of the song in which the performer(s) would be mentioned. To score correctly, you may use a song title only once.

71. Frank Sinatra   a. Bama Breeze

72. Mick Jagger   b. Miss You So Badly

73. Otis Redding   c. Wheel Inside the Wheel

74. Kiss   d. Cultural Infidel

75. Patsy Cline   e. Hello Texas

76. Village People   f. Meet Me in Memphis

77. Jan & Dean   g. Saxophones

78. Judy Garland   h. Mañana

79. Bee Gees   i. Making Music for Money

80. Dr. John   j. Domino College

    k. What If the Hokey Pokey is All It Really is About

    l. None

Answers are on the next page . . .

ANSWERS:

71. k: Frank Sinatra/What If the Hokey Pokey is All It Really is About

72. a: Mick Jagger/Bama Breeze

73. f: Otis Redding/Meet Me in Memphis

74. h: Kiss/Mañana

75. b: Patsy Cline/Miss You So Badly

76. d: Village People/Cultural Infidel

77. j: Jan & Dean/Domino College

78. c: Judy Garland/Wheel Inside the Wheel

79. e: Bee Gees/Hello Texas

80. g: Dr. John/Saxophones

 Things to Know by Chart:

PENSACOLA, FLORIDA
Latitude: 30° N
Longitude: 87° W

Dis & Dat / Number 5:

81. What can you learn to make with kindergarten toys?

82. Whose books did the old man read in the Pacific?

83. Where are the lights that do not shine for you?

84. What was broken in Spago's?

85. How many wheels are there on your blue and white travelin' machine?

86. Where did you stash the goods stolen from the Mini-Mart?

87. What did the sign read at His Majesty's Court Hotel?

88. How often could you drink cold champagne?

89. Who dances around the pool?

90. In which two songs do you mention your son, Cameron?

Answers are on the next page . . .

Answers:

81. Noise/QMN

82. James Jones/STOMH

83. In the harbor/SOH

84. Your nose/YNWIDBA

85. Nine/TRAV

86. In your coat and jeans/PBC

87. Praise His Name/TBIO

88. Nearly every night/HDO

89. Delaney/DTTS

90. False Echoes/FE; Beach House on the Moon/BHOTM

Things to Know by Chart:

LIVINGSTON, MONTANA
Latitude: 45° N
Longitude: 110° W

DIS & DAT / NUMBER 6:

91. Why did you go to Capt. Tony's?

92. What might a company make by punching holes in Vanilla Wafers?

93. What do you miss when you're gone?

94. What part of the day is like "an angel weeping"?

95. What two things cannot be trusted?

96. Who are the only ones who can see songlines?

97. What movie did Frank and Lola see?

98. What did the Russians and the sailors want to trade?

99. What is waiting just around the bend?

100. What part do you not want to play again?

Answers are on the next page . . .

ANSWERS:

91. To get out of the heat/LMIP

92. Your records/PAP

93. The water/THLAL

94. Sunset/PTC

95. Scales; clocks/OTWT

96. Dreamers/BS

97. Body Heat/FAL

98. Beer and plutoniom/ADR

99. The point of no return/BTB

100. The loser/PTLA

 Things to Know by Chart:

MARSEILLES, FRANCE
Latitude: 43° N
Longitude: 5° E

O
F
F

T
H
E

R
E
C
O
R
D

OFF THE RECORD / NUMBER 1:

This category of OTR questions ranges beyond just lyrics to a broader knowledge of Jimmy's creative work: in this case, movie soundtracks.

Correctly match the number of the motion picture with the letter of the song title which appears in that movie. To score correctly, you may use a song title only once.

OTR 1.	Hoot	a.	Hello Texas
OTR 2.	The Firm	b.	Ragtop Day
OTR 3.	FM	c.	Gulf coastal
OTR 4.	Contact	d.	Don't Bug Me
OTR 5.	Urban Cowboy	e.	Boomerang Love
OTR 6.	Summer Rental	f.	Survive
OTR 7.	The Slugger's Wife	g.	Stars on the Water
OTR 8.	Always	h.	Livingston Saturday Night
OTR 9.	Arachnophobia	i.	Turning Around
OTR 10.	Coast to Coast	j.	Purple People Eater
		k.	Good Guys Win
		l.	None

Answers are on the next page . . .

ANSWERS:

OTR 1.   k: Hoot/Good Guys Win

OTR 2.   g: The Firm/Stars on the Water

OTR 3.   h: FM/Livingston Saturday Night

OTR 4.   j: Contact/Purple People Easter

OTR 5.   a: Urban Cowboy/Hello Texas

OTR 6.   i: Summer Rental/Turning Around

OTR 7.   b: The Slugger's Wife/Ragtop Day

OTR 8.   e: Always/Boomerang Love

OTR 9.   d: Arachnophobia/Don't Bug Me

OTR 10.   f: Coast to Coast/Survive

INDECISIONS / NUMBER 2:

Life is not all just a choice between rhum and tequila. So, here's a variation on a good old TRUE/FALSE quiz.

Correctly label each of the following songs as mentioning either BEER or WINE based only upon the information provided in the recorded lyrics.

101. BEER/WINE: Great Filling Station Holdup

102. BEER/WINE: I Wish Lunch Could Last Forever

103. BEER/WINE: Changes in Latitudes, Changes in Attitudes

104. BEER/WINE: Last Mango in Paris

105. BEER/WINE: He Went to Paris

106. BEER/WINE: Gypsies in the Palace

107. BEER/WINE: Miss You So Badly

108. BEER/WINE: The Weather is Here, I Wish You Were Beautiful

109. BEER/WINE: Incommunicado

110. BEER/WINE: I Heard I Was in Town

Answers are on the next page . . .

ANSWERS:

101. Great Filling Station Holdup/BEER

102. I Wish Lunch Could Last Forever/WINE

103. Changes in Latitudes, Changes in Attitudes/WINE

104. Last Mango in Paris/BEER

105. He Went to Paris/WINE

106. Gypsies in the Palace/WINE

107. Miss You So Badly/BEER

108. The Weather is Here, I Wish You Were Beautiful/BEER

109. Incommunicado/BEER

110. I Heard I Was in Town/BEER

Things to Know by Chart:

CUMBERLAND PLATEAU, TENNESSEE
Latitude: 36° N
Longitude: 84° W

Don' chu know / number 4:

Correctly match the number of the writer with the letter of the song in which he is mentioned. To score correctly, you may use a song title only once.

111.	John MacDonald	a.	If It All Falls Down
112.	Oscar Wilde	b.	Cultural Infidel
113.	James Joyce	c.	If I Could Just Get It on Paper
114.	James Jones	d.	Quietly Making Noise
115.	Ernest Hemingway	e.	Incommunicado
116.	Mark Twain	f.	Who's the Blonde Stranger
117.	William Faulkner	g.	Barometer Soup
118.	Louis L'Amour	h.	Far Side of the World
119.	Stephen King	i.	Sending the Old Man Home
120.	Antoine de Saint-Exupéry	j.	That's What Living is to Me
		k.	Vampires, Mummies & the Holy Ghost
		l.	None

Answers are on the next page . . .

ANSWERS:

111.   e: John MacDonald/Incommunicado

112.   d: Oscar Wilde/Quietly Making Noise

113.   a: James Joyce/If It All Falls Down

114.   i: James Jones/Sending the Old Man Home

115.   b: Ernest Hemingway/Cultural Infidel

116.   j: Mark Twain/That's What Living is to Me
       [Note: Though Twain indeed did create the character of the Remit-
       tance Man in Following the Equator, as well as the term "barometer
       soup" in A Tramp Abroad, he is not mentioned in either song.]

117.   c: William Faulkner/If I Could Just Get It on Paper

118.   f: Louis L'Amour/Who's the Blonde Stranger?

119.   k: Stephen King/Vampires, Mummies & the Holy Ghost

120.   d: Antoine de Saint-Exupéry/Far Side of the World

 Things to Know by Chart:

YUKON TERRITORY, CANADA
Latitude: 63° N
Longitude: 135° W

Dis & Dat / Number 7:

121. Where do you hang your Christmas stocking in the Caribbean?

122. Where do you hang your stocking on Christmas Island?

123. Who spends Christmas on a hook?

124. What do you and Santa have in common in the Big Top?

125. What was the only thing you had to do a day or two ago?

126. What covers Santa's buns?

127. What has moved at near light speed?

128. Who would Santa like to be for the weekend?

129. What is the only thing they don't have in the Caribbean for Christmas?

130. What keeps drifting as the children sing and play?

Answers are on the next page . . .

ANSWERS:

121. The mast/CITC

122. A coconut tree/CHRISL

123. A sailor/ASC

124. You come around every year (ho ho ho)/BT

125. Drive on the left side/JB

126. Chimney scars/HHHAABOR

127. Your life/MCA/NFFH

128. Peter Pan/HHHAABOR

129. Snow/CITC

130. The continents/ASC

 Things to Know by Chart:

CEDAR KEY, FLORIDA
Latitude: 29° N
Longitude: 83° W

DIS & DAT / NUMBER 8:

131. How will you feel when you do fall?

132. Who saved the Jolly Mon?

133. Cotton candy hair, aluminum dimples, and cast iron curls are all traits of what sort of people?

134. What four items did you steal from the Mini-Mart?

135. What sort of animal has an unbendable barnacle brain?

136. What weapon does your partner wield in the Great Filling Station Holdup?

137. What two other words describe the young man who went to Paris?

138. Where did you nearly die after jumping off the boat?

139. What is your prayer in the middle of the night?

140. How much money did you give your hitchhiker?

Answers are on the next page . . .

ANSWERS:

131. To amend your carnivorous habits/CIP

132. Glad to go/DG

133. Northeast Texas Women/NTW

134. Peanut butter and a can of sardines/PBC

135. An old manatee/GOBNU

136. Pellet gun/GFSH

137. Impressive and aggressive/HWTP

138. Tampico/TT

139. Lord, let us out of this hall of mirrors/MOTN

140. Five dollars/WNGBG

 Things to Know by Chart:

RIO de JANEIRO, BRAZIL
Latitude: 22° S
Longitude: 43° W

Don' chu know / number 5:

Correctly match the number of the fruit with the letter of the song in which it is mentioned. To score correctly, you may use a song title only once.

141. Peach		a.	They Don't Dance Like Carmen No More
142. Banana		b.	Gravity Storm
143. Lime		c.	Fruitcakes
144. Mango		d.	Quietly Making Noise
145. Coconut		e.	Banana Republics
146. Grapefruit		f.	Caribbean Amphibian
147. Orange		g.	The Ballad of Skip Wiley
148. Pineapple		h.	Far Side of the World
149. Cherry		i.	Grapefruit-Juicyfruit
150. Apple		j.	Gypsies in the Palace
		k.	Nobody Speaks to the Captain No More
		l.	None

Answers are on the next page . . .

ANSWERS:

141. j: Peach/Gypsies In the Palace

142. h: Banana/Far Side of the World

143. e: Lime/Banana Republics

    [Note: Some will insist that Jimmy is singing the word "line" –
    as in "a line of cocaine" – which rhymes with the later lyric of
    "melody divine." Others will claim that he sings of "a bottle of
    rhum and a lime." So, for the purposes of this set of questions,
    we'll use the fruit.]

144. a: Mango/They Don't Dance Like Carmen No More

145. k: Coconut/Nobody Speaks to the Captain No More

146. i: Grapefruit/Grapefuit-Juicy Fruit

147. g: Orange/The Ballad of Skip Wiley

148. f: Pineapple/Caribbean Amphibian

149. l: Cherry/None

150. b: Apple/Gravity Storm

 Things to Know by Chart:

MONTSERRAT, WEST INDIES
Latitude: 16° N
Longitude: 62° W

Dis & Dat / Number 9:

151. What happens behind an occupied sign, in a rental car, and on a red-eye flight?

152. In Hollywood, what do they feed rather than their souls?

153. What shoes did you wear on the hood of a Cadillac?

154. Who is the handiest Frenchman in the Caribbean?

155. Where did Oscar Wilde die?

156. What do you miss more than you miss New Orleans?

157. Where does everybody expect you to show?

158. Whom does Salome toast with pink champagne?

159. What might fifteen get you?

160. What's behind the antics of a hopeless romantic?

Answers are on the next page . . .

Answers:

151.   Acts of love in decline/ʟɪᴅ

152.   Their egos/ᴏᴠᴋ

153.   Golf shoes/ꜱᴛꜱ

154.   Hippolyte Lamartine/ᴛʜꜰɪᴛᴄ

155.   In bed, above your head/Qᴍɴ

156.   The one you care for/ᴅʏᴋᴡɪᴍᴛᴍɴᴏ

157.   At the party/ᴡᴛᴘ

158.   Her trio/ᴡꜱᴘᴛᴅ

159.   Twenty/ʟꜱɴ

160.   A heart full of smiles/ʟɪᴄᴇ

 Things to Know by Chart:

SAN REMO, ITALY
Latitude: 43° N
Longitude: 7° E

DIS & DAT / NUMBER 10:

161. Who played pirate for a day?

162. Who was half woman/half child?

163. What are the three things which people say comprise your perfect life?

164. Where in Capt. Tony's were the old man's words written?

165. How might you kill off the hours and be somewhere you feel free?

166. If you know in your heart that you are a sailor, where is your ship?

167. If the hockey game is on, what is the temperature outside?

168. What did you do rather than enter the draft?

169. What's in the bottle carried by the good-looking blonde?

170. What venue near Austin is the site of mandolin playing?

Answers are on the next page . . .

ANSWERS:

161. Superstitious children/OTSTL

162. Marita/CCOP

163. Your kids, toys, and wife/JM

164. On the dingy wall of the head (bathroom)/LMIP

165. Sailing away in a boat on the sea/WILD

166. On the way/TA

167. Twenty degrees/BD

168. Earned a college degree/WATPOPWUA

169. Scotch/BIRI

170. A pasture/SSFAAM

 Things to Know by Chart:

LIVINGSTON, TEXAS
Latitude: 30° N
Longitude: 94° W

DON' CHU KNOW / NUMBER 6:

Correctly match the number of the weather condition with the letter of the song in which it is mentioned. To score correctly, you may use a song title only once.

171.	Squall	a.	Mañana
172.	Blizzard	b.	Volcano
173.	Haze	c.	Fruitcakes
174.	Breeze	d.	Quietly Making Noise
175.	Snow	e.	Trying to Reason with Hurricane Season
176.	Lightning	f.	Come Monday
177.	Waterspouts	g.	Barefoot Children in the Rain
178.	Monsoon	h.	Growing Older But Not Up
179.	Winds	i.	Migration
180.	Thunder	j.	Banana Wind
		k.	Bob Roberts Society Band
		l.	None

Answers are on the next page . . .

ANSWERS:

171. i: Squall/Migration

172. d: Blizzard/Quietly Making Noise

173. f: Haze/Come Monday

174. k: Breeze/Bob Roberts Society Band

175. a: Snow/Mañana

176. c: Lightning/Fruitcakes

177. e: Waterspouts/Trying to Reason with Hurricane Season

178. b: Monsoon/Volcano

179. h: Winds/Growing Older But Not Up

        [Of course, if you selected Banana Wind for this answer, then
        you are not following directions. You must select the song lyric in
        which this weather condition is mentioned. As an instrumental,
        Banana Wind has no lyrics.]

180. g: Thunder/Barefoot Children in the Rain

Things to Know by Chart:

PASCAGOULA, MISSISSIPPI
Latitude: 30° N
Longitude: 88° W

DIS & DAT / NUMBER 11:

181. What do you wish would blow away your worries?

182. What did Frank and Lola count in their sleep?

183. What is the difference between shells and dreams?

184. What sort of beverage makes you quite immobile?

185. What might enable you to solve mysteries, too?

186. Name three things that excite you.

187. Where did Merita come from?

188. Where did you see the former lion tamer and the former high wire act now living?

189. What is just about your favorite thrill?

190. If you lunched with your boyfriends, what might the girls discuss?

Answers are on the next page . . .

ANSWERS:

181. Christmas winds/LP

182. He counted sheep; she, rainbows/FAL

183. Shells sink; dreams float/DTTS

184. Whiskey/BF

185. A pencil thin mustache/PTM

186. Pastry, lobster, love/TWAIK

187. The coast/CCOP

188. Under the bridge/MB

189. Landing your plane in the water/JM

190. Cigars/FAB

Things to Know by Chart:

DISNEYLAND, CALIFORNIA
Latitude: 33° N
Longitude: 118° W

DIS & DAT / NUMBER 12:

191. What yardwork did the captain do in his retirement?

192. What sort of distressed persons are in condos?

193. What does life as a jester keep you doing?

194. What kind of crowd might you find at the Blue Heaven?

195. What did some unscrupulous mind add to the shaker of things S/He collected?

196. What do the nautical wheelers call themselves?

197. What tatoo image is a permanent reminder?

198. What will you do when a long-awaited car drives by?

199. What are full of secrets?

200. What is the name of your co-conspirator at the Mini-Mart?

Answers are on the next page . . .

ANSWERS:

191. Raking leaves in the backyard/TCATK

192. Damsels/GITP

193. Moving around/SOAS

194. Flashback/BHR

195. Ice/SBH

196. Sailors/NW

197. Indian chief poised for attack/PROATF

198. Wave hello/NFN

199. The hills/ATWIWY

200. Ricky/PBC

Things to Know by Chart:

DUVALIER AIRPORT, HAITI
Latitude: 18° N
Longitude: 72° W

INDECISIONS / NUMBER 3:

Okay, the first ten questions in this book asked you to identify songs included in Songs You Know by Heart. But I didn't give you a chance to identify ALL those songs. So, from the list below, identify the remaining songs are included on that collection of greatest hit(s)?

201. YES/NO: Last Mango in Paris

202. YES/NO: Boat Drinks

203. YES/NO: He Went to Paris

204. YES/NO: Honey Do

205. YES/NO: Son of A Son of A Sailor

206. YES/NO: Cheeseburger in Paradise

207. YES/NO: Why Don't We Get Drunk and Screw

208. YES/NO: Pencil Thin Mustache

209. YES/NO: Havana Daydreamin'

210. YES/NO: Margaritaville

Answers are on the next page . . .

Answers:

201. Last Mango in Paris/NO!
     [How many times must I tell you this?]

202. Boat Drinks/YES

203. He Went to Paris/YES
     [This is probably the Paris song that you're looking for.]

204. Honey Do/NO

205. Son of A Son of A Sailor/YES

206. Cheeseburger in Paradise/YES

207. Why Don't We Get Drunk and Screw/YES

208. Pencil Thin Mustache/YES

209. Havana Daydreamin'/NO

210. Margaritaville/YES (DUH!)

Things to Know by Chart:

LEADVILLE, COLORADO
Latitude: 39° N
Longitude: 106° W

Don' chu know / number 7:

Correctly match the number of the source of music with the letter of the song in which it is mentioned. To score correctly, you may use a song title only once.

211.	Gramophone	a.	Creola
212.	RCA Victrola	b.	Survive
213.	78 (rpm records)	c.	She's Got You
214.	Transistor radio	d.	Homemade Music
215.	Internet	e.	Woman Going Crazy on Caroline Street
216.	Tapes	f.	Gypsies in the Palace
217.	Stereo	g.	Brown-Eyed Girl
218.	Jukebox	h.	Fruitcakes
219.	Records	i.	Holiday
220.	CDs	j.	Frenchman for the Night
		k.	The Wino and I Know
		l.	None

Answers are on the next page . . .

ANSWERS:

211. j.   Gramophone/Frenchman for the Night

212. a: RCA Victrola/Creola

213. k: 78 (rpm records)/The Wino and I Know

214. g: Transistor radio/Brown-Eyed Girl

215. i: Internet/Holiday

216. h: Tapes/Fruitcakes

217. b: Stereo/Survive

218. e: Jukebox/Woman Going Crazy on Caroline Street

219. c: Records/She's Got You

220. d: CDs/Homemade Music

 Things to Know by Chart:

HAVANA, CUBA
Latitude: 23° N
Longitude: 82° W

DIS & DAT / NUMBER 13:

221. What is the radically cheap form of therapy?

222. While you're vacantly occupied, where is your honey?

223. In what building might you find the Order of the Sleepless Knights?

224. Who is on Cedar Key?

225. Upon what continent are you searching for the spirit of the great heart?

226. What do the Nautical Wheelers call themselves?

227. Who has Spider John gone searching for?

228. Who ran into the (Great) wall (of China)?

229. What kind of watch do you buy your baby on a shopping spree?

230. To what does the Remittance Man recite his confessions?

Answers are on the next page . . .

ANSWERS:

221. Poppin' bubble wrap/IDKAIDC

222. Up in South Carolina/HDO

223. In the palace/GITP

224. Travis McGee/INC

225. Africa/GH

226. Sailors/NW

227. Lily (Diamond Lill)/BOSJ

228. Marco Polo/SOC

229. Space Age/LS

230. Seagulls; loons/RM

Things to Know by Chart:

BORA BORA, LEEWARD SOCIETY ISLANDS
Latitude: 17° S
Longitude: 145° W

DIS & DAT / NUMBER 14:

231. What costs a quarter to make you feel alright?

232. What type of songs does your agent say that people buy?

233. What would you rather do than talk with your shrink?

234. Who wears alligator shirts?

235. What nearly ran over Frank and Lola?

236. What business does the brand new country star plan to open in his hometown?

237. What is General Electric doing?

238. What did the Jolly Mon hear on his way home?

239. How do the gypsies get at the good stuff in the closet?

240. What are you willing to do with the rest of everything you own?

Answers are on the next page . . .

ANSWERS:

231. Magic Fingers/THR

232. Love songs/MMFM

233. Walk through fire/VMATHG

234. The foursome on the golf course/POT

235. The lifeguard's Jeep/FAL

236. A chain of bowling alleys/BNCS

237. Their best/MAN

238. A cry for help/JMS

239. Shoot the lock off/GITP

240. Give it up/IHFMAH

 Things to Know by Chart:

SHANGHAI, CHINA
Latitude: 31° N
Longitude: 121° E

Don' chu know / number 8:

Correctly match the number of the dance with the letter of the song in which it is mentioned. To score correctly, you may use a song title only once.

241.	Bear Dance	a.	Overkill
242.	Rhumba	b.	First Look
243.	Cajun Dance	c.	If It All Falls Down
244.	Snake Dance	d.	Big Top
245.	Corporate Dance	e.	Honey Do
246.	Conga Line	f.	Lone Palm
247.	Samba	g.	Livingston Saturday Night
248.	Tango	h.	God's Own Drunk
249.	Jitterbug	i.	Gypsies in the Palace
250.	Ladies' Choice	j.	Bob Roberts Society Band
		k.	Pascagoula Run
		l.	None

Answers are on the next page . . .

ANSWERS:

241. h: Bear Dance/God's Own Drunk

242. d: Rhumba/Big Top

243. k: Cajun Dance/Pascagoula Run

244. c: Snake Dance/If It All Falls Down

245. a: Corporate Dance/Overkill

246. i: Conga Line/Gypsies in the Palace

247. b: Samba/First Look

248. f: Tango/Lone Palm

249. j: Jitterbug/Bob Roberts Society Band

250. e: Ladies' Choice/Honey Do

 Things to Know by Chart:

MARGARITAVILLE, LOUISIANA
Latitude: 30° N
Longitude: 90° W

Dis & DAT / NUMBER 15:

251. What two actresses are named in different versions of Landfall?

252. Which song originally says you suffered a cut heal, but in later versions says you suffered a broken leg.

253. Which song title is a Polynesian phrase?

254. What sort of people look the same in the city?

2525. What instrument causes a crowd to go deaf and dumb?

256. Why did the Twelve-Volt Man go to Mexico?

257. What did you get in a bar on Bourbon Street?

258. If the phone doesn't ring, where will you be?

259. Where might you have met an African prancer?

260. As a kid, what chance did you never miss?

Answers are on the next page . . .

ANSWERS:

251. Lucille Ball in the original Changes in Latitudes, Changes in Attitudes version; Lauren Bacall in a subsequent version on You Had To Be There

252. Margaritaville/MAR

253. Mele Kalikimaka/MK

254. The dudes and the dykes/DVL

2525. Salome's drum/WSPTD

256. To work on his tan/TVM

257. Your very first scar/TWAIK

258. In the eye of the storm/ITPDRIM

259. In the Metro/QMN

260. To climb upon the captain's knee and hear sea tales/TCATK

Things to Know by Chart:

THREE MILE ISLAND, PENNSYLVANIA
Latitude: 38° N
Longitude: 78° W

DIS & DAT / NUMBER 16:

261. What resembled a huge, golden opal?

262. In what song might one find a harpoon man?

263. Where do airport customs hassle you?

264. Who should be sent to French Guiana?

265. What sorts of books have you read?

266. Where did Jesus stash his trash?

267. Where did the old man serve in the Navy?

268. What is Beggar's Tomb?

269. Where might you see the gypsy and the fool?

270. What is it that truth is stranger than?

Answers are on the next page . . .

ANSWERS:

261. Your brother-in-law's still/GOD

262. Livingston Saturday Night/LSN

263. San Juan/VOL

264. Fat person man/FPM

265. About heroes and crooks/SOASOAS

266. Ecuador/HDA

267. The Pacific/STOMH

268. A silver mine/UJB

269. In the mirror/EOTR

270. Fishing/WTTWD

Things to Know by Chart:

BEIRUT, LEBANON
Latitude: 33° N
Longitude: 35° E

Don' chu know / number 9:

Correctly match the number of the sport with the letter of the song in which it is mentioned. To score correctly, you may use a song title only once.

271.	Hockey	a.	We are the People Our Parent Warned Us About
272.	Football	b.	A Pirate Looks at Forty
273.	Pool	c.	Twelve-Volt Man
274.	Rodeo	d.	Six-string Music
275.	Surfing	e.	Coconut Telegraph
276.	Sailing	f.	Boat Drinks
277.	Swimming	g.	Only Time Will Tell
278.	Fishing	h.	Banana Republics
279.	Baseball	i.	Schoolboy Heart
280.	Golf	j.	Brahma Fear
		k.	Livingston Saturday Night
		l.	None

Answers are on the next page . . .

ANSWERS:

271. f: Hockey/Boat Drinks

272. g: Football/Only Time Will Tell

273. k: Pool/Livingston Saturday Night

274. j: Rodeo/Brahma Fear

275. i: Surfing/Schoolboy Heart

276. h: Sailing/Banana Republics

277. d: Swimming/Six-string Music

278. b: Fishing/A Pirate Looks at Forty

279. c: Baseball/Twelve-Volt Man

280. a: Golf/We are the People Our Parents Warned Us About

Things to Know by Chart:

SPORTY'S AIRPORT/OHIO
Latitude: 39° N
Longitude: 84° W

Dis & Dat / Number 17:

281. Where did your hitchhiker come from?

282. Where was Billy Voltaire from?

283. What was the only protection in Africa for the old man whom you met in Capt. Tony's?

284. What sensuous treat appears in your dreams?

285. What smothers the Keys?

286. Who was trying to smell fear?

287. Who told you to "Keep your boots on"?

288. What is built upon mountains of memories?

289. What will you buy when you get off your long haul?

290. How long have you wanted to sail?

Answers are on the next page . . .

ANSWERS:

281. West Nashville/WNGBG

282. Miami way/CCOP

283. Swiss Army Knife/LMIP

284. Big warm bun and a huge hunk of meat/CIP

285. Mobile homes/MIG

286. The bear/GOD

287. Blonde stranger/WTBS

288. The City of Light (Paris)/QMN

289. A drink/CRWISL

290. Since you were three feet tall/APLAF

 Things to Know by Chart:

CREOLA, ALABAMA
Latitude: 30° N
Longitude: 88° W

Dis & Dat / Number 18:

291. What sort of Bar Mitvah did you perform at?

292. What sort of person's skin is white as paste?

293. Where might you find a woman whose lover abandoned her in Jamaica?

294. What country did Jesus fly to?

295. What do you plan to buy at Fausto's?

296. Where does the truthteller's son live?

297. After your car was stolen, what were you left to drive?

298. Who thumbed his nose at gravity?

299. If you had the wealth of the Aga Khan, what two items would you buy for every man, woman, and child?

300. In what state might one find Chinese modern lust?

Answers are on the next page . . .

ANSWERS:

291. A double/YNWIDBA

292. Cowboy/CITJ

293. Caroline Street/WGCOCS

294. Mexico/HDA

295. Chocolate milk/MHH

296. Nebraska/JAOTT

297. A nail/LMWANTD

298. Lindbergh/OAP

299. A mask and a snorkel/BSW

300. California/FRU

Things to Know by Chart:

MARTINIQUE, WEST INDIES
Latitude: 14° N
Longitude: 61° W

OFF THE RECORD / NUMBER 2:

Correctly match the number of the song title with the letter of the book written by Jimmy in which the song title also appears as a chapter title. To score correctly, you may use a song title MORE than once.

OTR 11. Happily Ever After,   a. Trouble Dolls
         Every Now and Then

OTR 12. Trouble on the Horizon   b. Tales from Margaritaville

OTR 13. I Wish Lunch Could Last   c. The Jolly Mon
         Forever

OTR 14. The Pascagoula Run   d. Where is Joe Merchant?

OTR 15. If I Had A Boat   e. A Pirate Looks at Fifty

OTR 16. Off to See the Lizard   f. A Salty Piece of Land

OTR 17. Take Another Road   g. Swine Not?

OTR 18. Changing Channels   h. None

OTR 19. That's My Story, and I'm Stickin' to It

OTR 20. No Plane on Sunday

Answers are on the next page . . .

ANSWERS:

OTR 11.   b: Happily Ever After, Now and Then/Where Is Joe Merchant?

OTR 12.   c: Trouble on the Horizon/A Pirate Looks at Fifty

OTR 13.   a: I Wish Lunch Could Last Forever/Tales from Margaritaville

OTR 14.   a: The Pascagoula Run/Tales from Margaritaville

OTR 15.   f: If I Had A Boat/A Salty Piece of Land

OTR 16.   a: Off to See the Lizard/Tales from Margaritaville

OTR 17.   a: Take Another Road/Tales from Margaritaville

OTR 18.   b: Changing Channels/Where Is Joe Merchant?

OTR 19.   b: That's My Story/Where Is Joe Merchant?

OTR 20.   b/c: No Plane On Sunday/Where Is Joe Merchant? and/or A Pirate Looks at Fifty

INDECISIONS / NUMBER 4:

Aside from the some of the obvious landfalls, Jimmy now and then mentions some other places. And more than a few are a stretch of the seafarer's imagination. So, correctly label whether each of the following places is either a TRUE reference from his songs or a FALSE reference, based only upon the information provided in the recorded lyrics.

301. TRUE/FALSE: The Kremlin

302. TRUE/FALSE: Yukon Territory

303. TRUE/FALSE: Yucatan Peninsula

304. TRUE/FALSE: Himalayas

305. TRUE/FALSE: Pauper's Hill

306. TRUE/FALSE: Nepal

307. TRUE/FALSE: Barbecue Hill

308. TRUE/FALSE: Sydney

309. TRUE/FALSE: Paraguay

310. TRUE/FALSE: Muscle Shoals

ANSWERS:

301. The Kremlin: TRUE/EM

302. Yukon Territory: TRUE/VOL

303. Yucatan: TRUE/LIU

304. Himalayas: TRUE/SOC & OVK

305. Pauper's Hill: TRUE/CCOP

306. Nepal: TRUE/LF

307. Barbecue Hill: TRUE/IWLCLF

308. Sydney: TRUE/RM

309. Paraguay: TRUE/CITJ

310. Muscle Shoals: TRUE/SFOA

 Things to Know by Chart:

NEW YORK CITY, NEW YORK
Latitude: 42° N
Longitude: 76° W

Don' chu know / number 10:

Correctly match the number of the drinking establishment with the letter of the song in which it is mentioned. To score correctly, you may use a song title only once.

311. Florabama

312. Spago's

313. Shipwreck Lounge

314. Blue Light

315. Chart Room

316. Le Bête à Z'ailes

317. Stateline Bar

318. Tonga Room

319. Snake Pit

320. BO's

a. Saxophones

b. Altered Boy

c. My Head Hurts, My Feet Stink and I Don't Love Jesus

d. Pascagoula Run

e. Turn Up the Heat and Chill the Rose

f. Ragtop Day

g. Why Don't We Get Drunk

h. Tampico Trauma

i. You'll Never Work in Dis Bidness Again

j. Clichés

k. Stars on the Water

l. None

Answers are on the next page . . .

ANSWERS:

311. f: Florabama/Ragtop Day

312. i: Spago's/You'll Never Work in Dis Bidness Again

313. a: Shipwreck Lounge/Saxophones

314. k: Blue Light/Stars on the Water

315. j: Chart Room/Clichés

316. e: Le Bête à Z'ailes/Turn Up the Heat and Chill the Rose

317. d: Stateline Bar/Pascagoula Run

318. b: Tonga Room/Altered Boy

319. c: Snake Pit/My Head Hurts, My Feet Stink, and I Don't Love Jesus

320. l: BO's/None

 Things to Know by Chart:

VINEYARD SOUND, MASSACHUSETTS
Latitude: 41° N
Longitude: 71° W

Dis & DAT / NUMBER 19:

321. What time should Snake plan to meet you at the airport tomorrow night?

322. How big do you estimate the body might be of that Kodiak bear?

323. How long has it been since the hitchhiker from Nashville last attended church?

324. What is the population of Ringling?

325. What sort of music do you describe as "elementary?"

326. For how many wild years did the party rock in L'Orient?

327. How many holes did you shoot in your freezer?

328. Which set is the lounge act playing in the casino?

329. How far are you from Le Select?

330. How many boat drinks do you need?

Answers are on the next page . . .

ANSWERS:

321. Ten/GITP

322. Twenty-seven acres/GOD

323. Thirty-six Sundays/WNGBG

324. Forty people/RR

325. Six-string/SSM

326. Five/ADR

327. Six/BD

328. Twenty-fourth/IMINFY

329. Ten thousand miles/TUTHCTR

330. Two more/BD

Things to Know by Chart:

PARIS, FRANCE
Latitude: 48° N
Longitude: 2° E

DIS & DAT / NUMBER 20:

331. Where is the bank of bad habits located?

332. Who is an annoying little gnat?

333. What bothered your wife most about your rasta me guests?

334. Who expected you to flip or fly?

335. Whose job is it to clean up the mess?

336. Which day do the hot lines again hum?

337. When you looked to the right of the stage, whom did you see take a bad fall?

338. How do you explain the likes of you?

339. Who is the girl of a thousand faces?

340. Based on your arith-a-matic, what be 3 plus 2?

Answers are on the next page . . .

ANSWERS:

331. In the corner of your soul/BOBH

332. Norman Paperman/HH(QMQ)

333. Their drumming after dinner/RA

334. The bear/GOD

335. The street sweeper/IMJ

336. Friday/COTE

337. The bass man/KIISW

338. Can't/OPH

339. Isabella/CC

340. Faux (pas)/TVM
      [Note: I am NOT about to explain puns to you that are based on both French AND Southernese. Either you get this one, or you don't. But I do hope you know that 3 plus 2 is really 5!]

Things to Know by Chart:

PORTOBELLO, BELIZE
Latitude: 17° N
Longitude: 88° W

DON' CHU KNOW / NUMBER 11:

Correctly match the number of the mind-altering substance with the letter of the song in which it is mentioned. To score correctly, you may use a song title only once.

341. Marijuana   a. Mañana

342. Darvon   b. Jamaica Mistaica

343. Dope   c. Presents to Send You

344. Quaalude   d. Pencil Thin Mustache

345. Ganja   e. Fool Button

346. Spliff cigar   f. Bama Breeze

347. Eskatrol   g. A Pirate Looks at Forty

348. Joint   h. My Head Hurts, My Feet Stink, and I Don't Love Jesus

349. Lid   i. We are the People Our Parents Warned Us About

350. Grass   j. Reggae Accident

   k. Please Take Your Drunken 15-Year-Old Girlfriend Home

   l. None

Answers are on the next page . . .

ANSWERS:

341. d: Marijuana/Pencil Thin Mustache

342. h: Darvon/My Head Hurts, My Feet Stink, and I Don't Love Jesus

343. a: Dope/Mañana

344. k: Quaalude/Please Take Your Drunken 15-Year-Old Girl-friend Home

345. b: Ganja/Jamaica Mistaica

346. j: Spliff cigar/Reggae Accident

347. e: Eskatrol/Fool Button

348. f: Joint/Bama Breeze

349. c: Lid/Presents to Send You

350. g: Grass/A Pirate Looks at Forty

 Things to Know by Chart:

HIMALAYA MOUNTAINS, ASIA
Latitude: 29° N
Longitude: 84° E

Dis & DAT / NUMBER 21:

351. What other word best describes the unscrupulous mind?

352. With what does the boy near Biloxi fill his pail?

353. Whom has Captain America bypassed?

354. When do you sit alone and think of your girl?

355. How many hangers are there in this hotel room?

356. If your life were that simple, where would you live?

357. How long did you used to go crazy?

358. If you had Cadillacs in your future, what did you have in your past?

359. What might betray you?

360. If you cruise to the gulf in your ragtop, what kind of music will you listen to?

Answers are on the next page . . .

ANSWERS:

351. Obscene/SBH

352. Salty water/BIL

353. The Lone Ranger/CA

354. When the day is done/BTTI

355. Thirty-two/THR

356. In the past/ITPDRIM

357. For days at a time/SOAS

358. Debutantes and/or money/IUTHMOT

359. The wild life/WTWLBM

360. Western music/RTD

 Things to Know by Chart:

DEATH VALLEY, CALIFORNIA
Latitude: 36° N
Longitude: 116° W

Dis & DAT / NUMBER 22:

361. What sort of work might you have done by mistake?

362. On what day does all the juicy news cease?

363. Of what country do you say that you've never really been to, but you'd sure like to go?

364. What message flashes on your laptop?

365. How many oysters did Frank and Lola eat?

366. Not wearing any underwear might be a sign of what condition?

367. What must you help Ellis do?

368. What night did you spend in Tijuana?

369. What sort of music does the ice cream man enjoy?

370. What is piled across from the bar in Ringling?

Answers are on the next page . . .

ANSWERS:

361. Manual labor/IMJ

362. Humpday (Wednesday)/COTE

363. Mexico/MEX

364. Today: therapy/VMATHG

365. A dozen each/FAL

366. Getting old/PTM

367. Get free/ED

368. Halloween/DS/HIT

369. Hillbilly (Hank Snow)/TWAIK

370. Beer cans/RR

Things to Know by Chart:

NEGRIL, JAMAICA
Latitude: 18° N
Longitude: 77° W

Don' chu know / number 12:

Correctly match the number of the land transportation with the letter of the song in which it is mentioned. To score correctly, you may use a song title only once.

371.	Nash	a.	Fool Button
372.	Lincoln Continental	b.	Where's the Party
373.	Hot rod Ford	c.	Reggae Accident
374.	Cordoba	d.	Big Rig
375.	Mustang	e.	Brand New Country Star
376.	Coupe de Ville	f.	Pascagoula Run
377.	Packard	g.	Tonight I Just Need My Guitar
378.	Jaguar	h.	Hey Good Lookin'
379.	Rambler	i.	Quietly Making Noise
380.	Cadillac	j.	Tin Cup Chalice
		k.	I Use to Have Money One Time
		l.	None

Answers are on the next page . . .

ANSWERS:

371. g: Nash/Tonight I Just Need My Guitar

372. e: Lincoln Continental/Brand New Country Star

373. h: Hot rod Ford/Hey Good Lookin'

374. a: Cordoba/Fool Button

375. i: Mustang/Quietly Making Noise

376. b: Coupe de Ville/Where's the Party?

377. j: Packard/Tin Cup Chalice

378. f: Jaguar/Pascagoula Run

379. c: Rambler/Reggae Accident

380. k: Cadillac/I Used to Have Money One Time

 Things to Know by Chart:

MEMPHIS, TENNESSEE
Latitude: 35° N
Longitude: 90° W

DIS & DAT / NUMBER 23:

381. What does the mermaid bring out in you?

382. Who would sneak a taste at the Sunday table?

383. Assuming it has a bed, what other amenities can be found in a room at the Tavernier Hotel?

384. After going through the Milky Way, where did young Mr. Moon and Magnus fly?

385. How do you treat your body?

386. What did Livingston learn in Texas?

387. What lures Americans to the banana republics?

388. When did you leave for Tampico?

389. What type of stories do the surgeons exchange?

390. What is love doing in the middle of the night?

Answers are on the next page . . .

ANSWERS:

381. The crustacean/MITN

382. Papa T/CRE

383. Fridge; phone/MMIM

384. Around Venus; around Mars (twice)/CPLPE

385. Like a tent/FRU

386. To be a cowboy; to rope and ride/LGTT

387. The sea/BARE

388. July/TT

389. Physician stories/MYSB

390. Spawning/MOTN

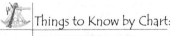

Things to Know by Chart:

GULF OF SIDRA, LYBIA
Latitude: 31° N
Longitude: 18° E

DIS & DAT / NUMBER 24:

391. How long did the man stay in Paris?

392. If the sky is red toward New Orleans, where might you be?

393. What things are the expatriated Americans running?

394. Where is Fruitcake City?

395. What do the ladies at the Stateline Bar wish to buy?

396. How long has Emma Mae been cooking at the DixieDiner?

397. How do men compensate for their lack of love and understanding?

398. Where might you head if you can't find some girl to help you spend your money?

399. What three things should never be described unless they have been seen?

400. Where did you park cars?

Answers are on the next page . . .

ANSWERS:

391. The steam whistle's blowing/STE

392. Biloxi/BIL

393. Depending upon your version of the song, they are either running "guns in," or running "ganja" (marijuana)/BARE

394. New York/FRU

395. They want to buy you a beer/TPR

396. Forty-eight years/DD

397. Stupidity/SS

398. Key West/ASN

399. The ocean; scenery; Kiss concert/MAN

400. At the Rainbow/YNWIDBA

 Things to Know by Chart:

BUFFALO, NEW YORK
Latitude: 42° N
Longitude: 78° W

INDECISIONS / NUMBER 5:

Correctly label each of the following song titles either RHUM (mentioned) or NONE (NOT mentioned) based only upon the information provided in the recorded lyrics.

401. RHUM/NONE: Far Side of the World

402. RHUM/NONE: Bank of Bad Habits

403. RHUM/NONE: Cowboy in the Jungle

404. RHUM/NONE: First Look

405. RHUM/NONE: Banana Republics

406. RHUM/NONE: A Lot to Drink About

407. RHUM/NONE: Volcano

408. RHUM/NONE: Lovely Cruise

409. RHUM/NONE: Son of a Son of a Sailor

410. RHUM/NONE: Fins

Answers are on the next page . . .

ANSWERS:

401. Far Side of the World/RHUM

402. Bank of Bad Habits/RHUM

403. Cowboy in the Jungle/RHUM

404. First Look/NONE

405. Banana Republics/RHUM

406. A Lot to Drink About/RHUM

407. Volcano/RHUM

408. Lovely Cruise/NONE

409. Son of a Son of a Sailor/RHUM

410. Fins/NONE

 Things to Know by Chart:

BRIDGETOWN, BARBADOS
Latitude: 13° N
Longitude: 59° W

Don' chu know / number 13:

Correctly match the number of the brand name product with the letter of the song in which it is mentioned. To score correctly, you may use a song title only once.

411. Weather Channel   a. Everybody's on the Phone

412. Tuborg Beer   b. The Ballad of Skip Wiley

413. Lincoln Logs   c. Holiday

414. Coke   d. I Will Play for Gumbo

415. Sears Tools   e. That's What Living is to Me

416. Blockbuster   f. Carnival World

417. Snickers   g. Great Filling Station Holdup

418. STP   h. Miss You So Badly

419. Krispy Kremes   i. Dreamsicle

420. Swatches   j. Peanut Butter Conspiracy

                           k. What If the Hokey Pokey is All It Really is About

                           l. None

Answers are on the next page . . .

ANSWERS:

411. c: Weather Channel/Holiday

412. h: Tuborg Beer/Miss You So Badly

413. a: Lincoln Logs/Everybody's on the Phone

414. k: Coke/What If the Hokey Pokey is All It Really is About

415. i: Sears Tools/Dreamsicle

416. b: Blockbuster/The Ballad of Skip Wiley

417. e: Snickers/That's What Living is to Me

418. g: STP/Great Filling Station Holdup

419. d: Krispy Kremes/I Will Play for Gumbo

420. f: Swatches/Carnival World

 Things to Know by Chart:

LONG ISLAND SOUND, NEW YORK/CONNECTICUT
Latitude: 41° N
Longitude: 73° W

DIS & DAT / NUMBER 25:

421. What's the status of your metabolic rate?

422. What effect does the phone bill sometimes have upon you?

423. Where might you find water in your shoes?

424. How might you describe the ladies where you have found your new home?

425. Where do wrinkles only go?

426. What sort of music should be on the radio, but is not?

427. Aside from the volcano, what else do they say is bound to blow?

428. What is it these days that borders on desire?

429. What do they plan to do with the whole damn fleet?

430. What instrument does your one-man band play?

Answers are on the next page . . .

ANSWERS:

421. It's pleasantly stuck/GOBNU

422. Makes you ill/SUR

423. A lovely cruise/LC

424. Not demanding/IHFMAH

425. Where smiles have been/BCITR

426. Homemade music/HM

427. This universe/APO

428. Need/TIJNMG

429. Send it into mothballs/STOMH

430. Guitar/TIJMG

 Things to Know by Chart:

TAMPICO, MEXICO
Latitude: 22° N
Longitude: 97° W

DIS & DAT / NUMBER 26:

431. Who called Customs?

432. Who guzzles twenty-five cent beers?

433. What type of girlfriend did you have as a kid?

434. What did Frank and Lola seek?

435. What did you do to the sharks off the Alabama shore?

436. Where might you find men with knives and scars?

437. What part of Texas was never like this?

438. Of whom are you the CEO?

439. What was the date of your dad's first birthday?

440. What do you want every now and then?

Answers are on the next page . . .

ANSWERS:

431. The gringo in the garden/EGACIM

432. The woman on Caroline Street/WGCOCS

433. Hippie/HM

434. A little privacy/FAL

435. Cussed at them/SIAH

436. In the Stateline Bar on the Pascagoula run/TPR

437. The west side/WTBS

438. The mailroom clerks/POW

439. Twenty-fifth of November, 1921/FE

440. To live happily ever after/HEA(NAT)

Things to Know by Chart:

CINCINNATI, OHIO
Latitude: 39° N
Longitude: 84° W

DON' CHU KNOW / NUMBER 14:

Correctly match the number of the watercraft with the letter of the song in which it is mentioned. To score correctly, you may use a song title only once.

441. Gunboat
442. Whaler boat
443. Barkentine
444. Riverboat
445. Freighter
446. Dhow
447. Sloop
448. Steamer
449. Shrimp boat
450. Iron ship

a. Everybody's Got a Cousin in Miami
b. Barefoot Children in the Rain
c. Beach House on the Moon
d. Nobody Speaks to the Captain No More
e. Brahma Fear
f. Tin Cup Chalice
g. Nautical Wheelers
h. The Captain and the Kid
i. Barometer Soup
j. Big Rig
k. He Went to Paris
l. None

Answers are on the next page . . .

ANSWERS:

441. a: Gunboat/Everybody's Got a Cousin in Miami

442. e: Whaler boat/Brahma Fear

443. h: Barkentine/The Captain and the Kid

444. b: Riverboat/Barefoot Children in the Rain

445. k: Freighter/He Went to Paris

446. c: Dhow/Beach House on the Moon

447. i: Sloop/Barometer Soup

448. l: Steamer/None
     [Note: Even though a nautical wheeler was a steam-powered
     paddle boat, it never mentions that. The songs which do tell
     of steamers are A Pirate Looks at Forty and Steamer.]

449. f: Shrimp boat/Tin Cup Chalice

450. d: Iron ship/Nobody Speaks to the Captain No More

 Things to Know by Chart:

YUCATÁN, MEXICO
Latitude: 21° N
Longitude: 86° W

DIS & DAT / NUMBER 27:

451. Standing ass-high in the rain, what city do you long for?

452. What is the anchor tied by a silver chain?

453. What is cheaper than water on Kinja?

454. What happened to the younger women?

455. Where do some folks paddle?

456. Who's a bore?

457. Where else would rather be than here?

458. Which of your muscles were rarely ever used?

459. How is the railroad lady now traveling?

460. Where were you when Steve Martin called?

Answers are on the next page . . .

ANSWERS:

451. Boston/CHD

452. Your love/SOCR

453. Champagne/CS,AN

454. You ran them away, but they came back/APLAF

455. In a lake/SSM

456. Your girlfriend/TWIHIWYWB

457. Sipping beer in some honky-tonk/GFSH

458. Those that controlled your smile/TNTAHT

459. By bus/RL

460. Sitting in a marina/MAN

Things to Know by Chart:

LONDON, ENGLAND
Latitude: 51° N
Longitude: 0° W

DIS & DAT / NUMBER 28:

461. What might make one throw down the luggage and stomp around?

462. What sort of simple protoplasm pays no rent?

463. How much would you give a 15-year-old toward a twenty-dollar cab fare?

464. What was the last word they told you that your woman said?

465. Who do you want to take you aboard the leaky Tiki?

466. How long might the wrong thing be the right thing?

467. Whom did the fellow's sister resemble?

468. What eatery is located on Tillman Street?

469. On the east side of what island are they still dancing with the stars?

470. What two observations might you make as you continue to be on your own?

Answers are on the next page . . .

Answers:

461. No plane on Sunday/NPOS

462. Jellyfish/MF

463. Thirty cents (for the bus)/PTYDFYOGH

464. England/ENG

465. Gardner McKay/WATPOPWUA

466. Until you lose control/BOBH

467. Frankenstein/ASN

468. The Dixie Diner/DD

469. Manhattan/ALTDA

470. The years grow shorter and the urge to move grows stronger/WWWEGH

 Things to Know by Chart:

PARAGUAY, SOUTH AMERICA
Latitude: 23° S
Longitude: 57° W

Don' chu know / number 15:

Correctly match the number of "the other song" with the letter of the song in which it is mentioned. To score correctly, you may use a song title only once.

471. Night Train

472. Dock of the Bay

473. La Vie en Rose

474. Jambalaya

475. Foxy Lady

476. Stormy Weather

477. Freebird

478. Save the Last Dance for Me

479. Twist and Shout

480. It's Raining, It's Pouring

a. Life is Just a Tire Swing

b. Barstool Boogie

c. Little Miss Magic

d. Prince of Tides

e. Meet Me in Memphis

f. Bama Breeze

g. We are the People Our Parents Warned Us About

h. Nobody Speaks to the Captain No More

i. You'll Never Work is Dis Bidness Again

j. Weather with You

k. Frenchman for the Night

l. None

Answers are on the next page . . .

ANSWERS:

471. b: Night Train/Barstool Boogie

472. e: Dock of the Bay/Meet Me in Memphis

473. k: La Vie en Rose/Frenchman for the Night

474. a: Jambalaya/Life is Just a Tire Swing

475. i: Foxy Lady/You'll Never Work in Dis Bidness Again

476. j: Stormy Weather/Weather with You

477. f: Freebird/Bama Breeze

478. d: Save the Last Dance for Me/Prince of Tides

479. g: Twist and Shout/We are the People Our Parents Warned Us About

480. c: It's Raining, It's Pouring/Little Miss Magic

 Things to Know by Chart:

DENVER, COLORADO
Latitude: 36° N
Longitude: 105° W

DIS & DAT / NUMBER 29:

481.   How are they making new movies these days?

482.   Who is making normal city people live above their means?

483.   Who is on the shore of this one particular harbor?

484.   What do you get as your hair turns gray?

485.   What is the California promise?

486.   What sort of girl comes from Buzios?

487.   How many times did you break your leg?

488.   What protects you from insects and vipers?

489.   Where does another road lead you?

490.   Where do you hear that you must face your fears?

Answers are on the next page . . .

ANSWERS:

481. In old black and white, with happy endings/PTM

482. The beautiful people in magazines/ITC

483. Playing children/OPH

484. Religion/CHR

485. I will never love another/CP

486. A third world girl/LMIP

487. Twice/MAR

488. Mosquito net/MF

489. To a hiding place/TAR

490. The songlines/OTSTL

 Things to Know by Chart:

THE KREMLIN, MOSCOW, RUSSIA
Latitude: 55° N
Longitude: 37° E

Dis & DAT / NUMBER 30:

491. What is it that changes like the weather?

492. What do you plan to build with your two hands?

493. With whom does a big old goofy man dance?

494. What do your friends say to your face?

495. How many ways do you know how to fail?

496. Where did you learn to fly at treetop level?

497. What will you find on an ancient chart?

498. What is the destination of the starship?

499. What sort of love goes from ninety to nothing?

500. What are you other than a sailor on a midnight sea?

Answers are on the next page . . .

ANSWERS:

491. Our lives/LMIP

492. A boat/BTOB

493. With a big old goofy girl/IABOGW

494. You're not yourself/SGOOMM

495. A million/BTTBOU

496. Vietnam/TF

497. Desert island/KOMH

498. The moon/CTTM

499. Love in decline/LID

500. A singer/BTB

Things to Know by Chart:

BEIJING. CHINA
Latitude: 39° N
Longitude: 166° E

OFF THE RECORD / NUMBER 3:

From the beginning of his recording career with ABC Records and on into the release of Fruitcakes on Margaritaville Records, Jimmy had performed in several videos that were intended to promote a specific project, but seldom were they visible anywhere. Anywhere, that is, until the release of Tales From MargaritaVision, which collected them together for Jimmy to introduce and put in context. So, let's go to the video!

OTR 31. Where was the Nautical Wheelers video filmed?

OTR 32. In which video does Jimmy not appear at all?

OTR 33. What is it that Joe Namath sells?

OTR 34. Which video was shot at the Islander Drive-In?

OTR 35. In what video does Jimmy peel off his moustache?

OTR 36. What beverage does Lola drink in bed?

OTR 37. What three letters are on Jimmy's cap in Tahiti?

OTR 38. What sort of performer is Bunny Briggs?

OTR 39. Where was Phil Clark tied up?

OTR 40. With what does Jimmy fill the rear seat of his convertible?

Answers are on the next page . . .

ANSWERS:

OTR 31. The Lantern Inn on Stock Island/NW

OTR 32. The He Went to Paris video shot in Philadelphia/HWTP

OTR 33. Hawaiian shirts/LIU

OTR 34. Take Another Road/TAR

OTR 35. His moustache is not real in Homemade Music/HM

OTR 36. Lola is drinking a bottle of Corona beer/WTBS

OTR 37. The cap is white with the letters USO, which stands for United Service Organizations/OPH

OTR 38. Jimmy calls Bunny Briggs "the world's greatest performing dancer."

OTR 39. Phil was tied to the Southeast Channel Marker/NW
[Note: Phil was not only a bartender at the Chart Room, but also the person about whom Jimmy wrote A Pirate Looks at Forty.]

OTR 40. Jimmy fills the rear seat with fruit and ice/LIU

CROSSING THE EQUATOR . . .

Now that you're midway through this collection of questions, you might not be quite certain whether you're down or you're up. So, this might be a good time to reposition yourself with some questions about the equator and its relative latitudes, including the tropics. Correctly mark each of the following songs as having some reference to these imaginary parallels (UP) or not (DOWN), based upon Jimmy's recorded lyrics.

EQ1. UP/DOWN: Cuban Crime of Passion

EQ2. UP/DOWN: Six-string Music

EQ3. UP/DOWN: Apocalypso

EQ4. UP/DOWN: Party at the End of the World

EQ5. UP/DOWN: Blue Heaven Rendezvous

EQ6. UP/DOWN: Banana Republics

EQ7. UP/DOWN: Happily Ever After (Now and Then)

EQ8. UP/DOWN: Everybody's Got A Cousin in Miami

EQ9. UP/DOWN: Migration

EQ10. UP/DOWN: Remittance Man

Answers are on the next page . . .

ANSWERS:

EQ1.   Cuban Crime of Passion/UP

EQ2.   Six-string Music/UP

EQ3.   Apocalypso/DOWN

EQ4.   Party at the End of the World/UP

EQ5.   Blue Heaven Rendezvous/UP

EQ6.   Banana Republics/UP

EQ7.   Happily Ever After (Now and Then)/UP

EQ8.   Everybody's Got A Cousin in Miami/UP

EQ9.   Migration/DOWN

EQ10. Remittance Man/UP

 Things to Know by Chart:

BUZZARDS BAY, MASSACHUSETTS
Latitude: 41° N
Longitude: 71° W

Don' chu know / number 16:

Correctly match the number of the body of water with the letter of the song in which it is mentioned. To score correctly, you may use a song title only once.

511. Sea of Cortez

512. River of Grass

513. Everglades

514. Rio Grande

515. Vineyard Sound

516. Lake Pontchartrain

517. Timber Bay

518. The Nile

519. Straits of Magellan

520. Buzzards Bay

a. Treetop Flyer

b. If I Could Just Get It on Paper

c. Breathe In, Breathe Out, Move On

d. Volcano

e. Everybody's Got a Cousin in Miami

f. Beach House on the Moon

g. Party at the End of the World

h. Distantly in Love

i. The Ballad of Skip Wiley

j. Lage Nom Ai

k. Treat Her Like a Lady

l. None

Answers are on the next page . . .

ANSWERS:

511. b: Sea of Cortez/If I Could Just Get It on Paper

512. e: River of Grass/Everybody's Got a Cousin in Miami

513. i: Everglades/The Ballad of Skip Wiley

514. a: Rio Grande/Treetop Flyer

515. j: Vineyard Sound/Lage Nom Ai

516. c: Lake Pontchartrain/Breathe In, Breathe Out, Move On

517. h: Timber Bay/Distantly in Love

518. f: The Nile/Beach House on the Moon

519. g: Straits of Magellan/Party at the End of the World

520. d: Buzzards Bay/Volcano

 Things to Know by Chart:

NASHVILLE, TENNESSEE
Latitude: 36° N
Longitude: 86° W

DIS & DAT / NUMBER 31:

521. What made you leave Tampico?

522. What sort of entertainment were the physicians off to see?

523. Whose fault is it really?

524. Which "babe" was asked if she could "add up all those bucks"?

525. What resolution do you make?

526. What sort of pains does the door-to-door salesman know?

527. What did the brand new country star no longer have on his car?

528. What sort of animals might not down your snowman in the meadow?

529. What was the price the unpopular poet's books?

530. What kind of person won't try to lead or follow?

Answers are on the next page . . .

ANSWERS:

521. You were thrown out for causing trouble/TT

522. A stripper/MYSB

523. Your own/CIP

524. The new Miss America/MASU

525. Never to make another [resolution]/TATS

526. Bell ringing/TWAIK

527. Steerhorns/BNCS

528. Alligators/WW

529. Four ninety-nine/DOAUP

530. The perfect partner/TPP

Things to Know by Chart:

ST. THOMAS, VIRGIN ISLANDS
Latitude: 18° N
Longitude: 64° W

DIS & DAT / NUMBER 32:

531. Who is the blond stranger?

532. What is the devil somewhere mixing?

533. Who operates the space station and bake shop?

534. What can undress a mademoiselle's heart?

535. What is the only thing to do to get along?

536. What did the quarters replace in your loafers?

537. Where did you used to rule the world?

538. How did the Jolly Mon earn his supper?

539. Where has Major Jim been looking for life?

540. Who is the blonde stranger?

Answers are on the next page . . .

ANSWERS:

531. Dan/WTBS

532. Fire and ice/SFYW

533. Desdemona/FRU

534. Violin/MVVD

535. Bend a little/BAL

536. Pennies/WATPOPWUA

537. From a payphone/OPH

538. Singing/JMS

539. On mars/WING

540. Marie/WTBS

Things to Know by Chart:

TIJUANA, MEXICO
Latitude: 32° N
Longitude: 117° W

DON' CHU KNOW / NUMBER 17:

Correctly match the number of the celebrity with the letter of the song in which it is mentioned. To score correctly, you may use a song title only once.

541.	Marilyn Monroe	a. Growing Older But Not Up
542.	Robin Leach	b. Baby's Gone Shopping
543.	Pete Rose	c. Simply Complicated
544.	Grant Wood	d. Fruitcakes
545.	Dr. Phil	e. Somewhere Over China
546.	Jerry Springer	f. King of Somewhere Hot
547.	Tony Orlando	g. Life is just a Tire Swing
548.	Marco Polo	h. A Mile High in Denver
549.	Stanley Kubrick	i. Morris' Nightmare
550.	John Wayne	j. Who's the Blonde Stranger
		k. License to Chill
		l. None

Answers are on the next page . . .

ANSWERS:

541.   b: Marilyn Monroe/Baby's Gone Shopping

542.   f: Robin Leach/King of Somewhere Hot

543.   a: Pete Rose/Growing Older But Not Up

544.   g: Grant Wood/Life is just a Tire Swing

545.   k: Dr. Phil/License to Chill

546.   c: Jerry Springer/Simply Complicated

547.   i: Tony Orlando/Morris' Nightmare

548.   e: Marco Polo/Somewhere Over China

549   d: Stanley Kubrick/Fruitcakes

550.   l: John Wayne/None
            [Note: If you picked h/A Mile High in Denver, you were at least
            thinking the right state. The correct song, though, would be
            Incommunicado, which tells of being on the Continental Divide
            when the Duke dies.]

Things to Know by Chart:

ZANZIBAR, TANZANIA
Latitude: 6° S
Longitude: 39° E

Dis & DAT / NUMBER 33:

551. Whom do you battle in Missoula?

552. Which maid is larger than life?

553. From what is that maid made?

554. What are the old folks and babies doing in the Middle of the Night?

555. Who was left behind with the fat maid in Ringling?

556. From what island was the maid wearing geckos around her neck?

557. What would that maid sing to bed?

558. What word should only be spoken with sincerity?

559. Where do you keep your "terminal daydream"?

560. What is "just a folly we can't see"?

Answers are on the next page . . .

ANSWERS:

551. Motel maids/MYSB

552. The mermaid/MITN

553. Holy water/MITH

554. Crying in the storm/MOTN

555. A cowboy and a dog/RR

556. Martinique/OTSTL

557. The sun/OTSTL

558. Mañana/MAN

559. In your backpack/IDK

560. Time/BG

Things to Know by Chart:

GULF OF GUINEA, AFRICA
Latitude: 0° N/S
Longitude: 0° E/W

DIS & DAT / NUMBER 34:

561. What has your lady made you understand?

562. What does Spooner now dine upon?

563. What sort of people sport guns and alibis?

564. What word best describes Desdemona's crew?

565. What did you buy after writing a note that said, "Be back in a minute?"

566. What did you study to prepare for your first look?

567. Where did you fear that you'll go if the floor caves in?

568. Who jumped from the old mahogany mill?

569. What did the fools pay to see in your front yard?

570. What would you rather do than live while you're dead?

Answers are on the next page . . .

ANSWERS:

561. A simple way of living/MLL

562. Steak and bacon/DOAUP

563. Coked-up cowboys/JM

564. Rookies/DBARS

565. Bought a boat and I sailed off in it/KD

566. All the language tapes/FL

567. Right straight to hell/TPR

568. The captain/NSTTCNM

569. A naked lady/THOG

570. Rather die while you're living/GOBNU

Things to Know by Chart:

SYDNEY, AUSTRALIA
Latitude: 33° S
Longitude: 151° E

Don' chu know / number 18:

Correctly match the number of the water creature with the letter of the song in which it is mentioned. To score correctly, you may use a song title only once.

571.	Tadpole	a.	Mental Floss
572.	Manatee	b.	Fins
573.	Jellyfish	c.	If I Could Just Get It on Paper
574.	Walrus	d.	Beautiful Swimmers
575.	Whale	e.	Growing Older But Not Up
576.	Squid	f.	Following the Equator
577.	Remora	g.	Bob Roberts Society Band
578.	Flying fish	h.	Treat Her Like a Lady
579.	Barracuda	i.	Stranded on a Sandbar
580.	Alligator	j.	That's What Living is to Me
		k.	Everybody's Got a Cousin in Miami
		l.	None

Answers are on the next page . . .

ANSWERS:

571. d: Tadpole/Beautiful Swimmers

572. e: Manatee/Growing Older But Not Up

573. a: Jellyfish/Mental Floss

574. j: Walrus/That's What Living is to Me

575. h: Whale/Treat Her Like a Lady

576. c: Squid/If I Could Just Get It on Paper

577. b: Remora/Fins

578. k: Flying fish/Everybody's Got a Cousin in Miami

579. l: Barracuda/None

580. g: Alligator/Bob Roberts Society Band

Things to Know by Chart:

LAGUNA, BRAZIL
Latitude: 28° S
Longitude: 48° W

Dis & DAT / NUMBER 35:

581. What instrument might make your music sound better?

582. What must one do to fight the good fight?

583. When speaking Southernese, what two letters give you trouble?

584. Whom might you find in a four-poster bed?

585. What country gave birth to a tribe of pyromaniacs?

586. Which mode of transportation is of no need?

587. Which cousin attended camp with you?

588. What does your brother-in-law ask you to watch?

589. Who was eating pasta at your dinner table?

590. What dinner would please you every day?

Answers are on the next page . . .

ANSWERS:

581. Saxophone/SABX

582. Go the distance/TGF

583. The two letters R and G/HDO

584. Someone to love/LUCST

585. China/WFTNE

586. The ten-speed/GF-JF

587. Baxter/LIJATS

588. His still/GOD

589. Four rasta men/RA

590. Oysters and beer/TCC

 Things to Know by Chart:

MUSCLE SHOALS, ALABAMA
Latitude: 34° N
Longitude: 87° W

DIS & DAT / NUMBER 36:

591.   Which drink are you on as the plane leaves the ground?

592.   How much jail time did the filling station holdup cost you?

593.   Who is going to learn to rhyme and to fly?

594.   In addition to your impure thoughts and smoking some, what other act did you include among your coastal confessions?

595.   Whatever became of your brother-in-law's still?

596.   What might you spend time converting nickels into?

597.   What is the name of Captain Adam Troy's vessel?

598.   Which beverage is a message in a bottle?

599.   What beverage did you swear never to drink again?

600.   What did you do to make Monty call on you?

Answers are on the next page . . .

ANSWERS:

591. Third/TWIHIWYWB

592. Two years/GFSH

593. Your daughter/LMM

594. Stealing peanut butter/COAC

595. The bear took it/GOD

596. Dimes/DCK

597. Kon Tiki/TBIO
    [Note: Though Gardner McKay played Capt. Adam Troy on ABCTV's "Adventures in Paradise" and though Capt. Troy's boat was called simply Tiki, for some reason Jimmy sings it as "Kon Tiki." In fact, however, Kon Tiki was the name of the primitive craft sailed across the Pacific on a 1947 expedition led by Thor Heyerdahl.]

598. Rose/TUTH

599. Tequila/PTSY

600. Grabbed him by the throat/DNT

Things to Know by Chart:

TRINIDAD, WEST INDIES
Latitude: 10° N
Longitude: 61° W

INDECISIONS / NUMBER 6:

This quick inventory gives you a chance to check your memory against the food items mentioned in Cheeseburger in Paradise. Correctly label each of the food items below as either TRUE (it's mentioned) or FALSE (it's NOT mentioned), based only upon the information provided in the recorded lyrics.

601. TRUE/FALSE: Heinz 57

602. TRUE/FALSE: Mustard

603. TRUE/FALSE: Onion

604. TRUE/FALSE: Salt

605. TRUE/FALSE: Lettuce

606. TRUE/FALSE: Bread

607. TRUE/FALSE: Meat

608. TRUE/FALSE: Cheddar

609. TRUE/FALSE: Bananas

610. TRUE/FALSE: Lime

Answers are on the next page . . .

Answers:

601. Heinz 57/TRUE

602. Mustard/FALSE
[Note: The phrase that Jimmy sings here is "muenster'd be nice," as in "muenster would be nice." To be sure, it might sound as though he's singing "mustard be nice," but here's the problem with that. If he were to say anything other than "muenster," then there would be no mention whatsoever of any cheese in a song about cheeseburgers.]

603. Onion/TRUE

604. Salt/FALSE

605. Lettuce/TRUE

606. Bread/TRUE

607. Meat/TRUE

608. Cheddar/FALSE

609. Bananas/TRUE

610. Lime/FALSE

Things to Know by Chart:

ANTIGUA, WEST INDIES
Latitude: 17° N
Longitude: 61° W

Don' chu know / number 19:

Correctly match the number of the entertainer with the letter of the song in which it is mentioned. To score correctly, you may use a song title only once.

611.	Stunt man	a.	Happily Ever After (Now & Then)
612.	Comedian	b.	The Night I Painted the Sky
613.	Actress	c.	Cuban Crime of Passion
614.	Stripper	d.	Holiday
615.	Guitar picker	e.	Off to See the Lizard
616.	Magician	f.	You'll Never Work in Dis Bidness Again
617.	Troubador	g.	Miss You So Badly
618.	Hemisphere dancer	h.	Quietly Making Noise
619.	Piano player	i.	He Went to Paris
620.	Vaudevillian	j.	Schoolboy Heart
		k.	Peanut Butter Conspiracy
		l.	None

Answers are on the next page . . .

ANSWERS:

611. a: Stunt man/Happily Ever After (Now & Then)

612. d: Comedian/Holiday

613. i: Actress/He Went to Paris

614. g: Stripper/Miss You So Badly

615. k: Guitar picker/Peanut Butter Conspiracy

616. b: Magician/The Night I Painted the Sky

617. e: Troubador/Off to See the Lizard

618. h: Hemisphere Dancer/Quietly Making Noise

619. c: Piano player/Cuban Crime of Passion

620. j: Vaudevillian/Schoolboy Heart

 Things to Know by Chart:

COLUMBUS, OHIO
Latitude: 39° N
Longitude: 83° W

DIS & DAT / NUMBER 37:

621. Where did Salome fly away to?

622. What might you be wearing in Communist China?

623. With what do you keep your craft well stocked?

624. How much moonshine did you drink?

625. What is your preferred mode of transportation where you have found a home?

626. Where might you learn how many years a mountain exists?

627. Why can't you book passage to the island?

628. Why did he go to Paris?

629. In "the lost verse" of Margaritaville, what do old men wear?

630. What is said by a voice from beyond the wind?

Answers are on the next page . . .

ANSWERS:

621. Rio/WSPTFD

622. Pajamas/CS,AN

623. Short stories; long laughs/BS

624. A whole jug/GOS

625. Old red bike/IHFMAH

626. The answer is blowin' in the wind/BITW

627. It has not ports/ISL

628. For answers/HWTP

629. Tank Tops/MAR

630. You must go beyond the end/BTE

 Things to Know by Chart:

SAIGON, SOUTH VIETNAM
Latitude: 12° N
Longitude: 106° E

Dis & DAT / NUMBER 38:

631. In their original version of Southern Cross, Crosby, Stills & Nash rhyme the words "trusted" and "busted," but what two words does Jimmy rhyme in their place?

632. Which wind are you backing off of?

633. Where would you like to set down the space shuttle?

634. What two presents does Rudolph go after?

635. What does the ornithologist lady say of the strange bird?

636. What is the eighth deadly sin?

637. What sort of people are fleeing the IRS?

638. What occupation suffers from a shortage?

639. Like what other animal do you feel you are in danger of extinction?

640. Which day was Africa Day in Amerigo?

Answers are on the next page . . .

ANSWERS:

631. "Tasted" and "basted"/sc

632. Northeast/ET

633. San Francisco/soc

634. A guitar and a Barbie doll/RRR

635. That he has wings on his heart/sB

636. Pizza!/BOBH

637. Expatriated Americans/BARE

638. Calypso poet/IIAFD

639. Whale/THLAL

640. Carnival/FD

Things to Know by Chart:

MARGARITAVILLE, SOUTH CAROLINA
Latitude: 32° N
Longitude: 79° W

Don' chu know / number 20:

Correctly match the number of the fictional character with the letter of the song in which it is mentioned. To score correctly, you may use a song title only once.

641. Snake
642. Liberty Valance
643. John Henry
644. Frankenstein
645. Zorro
646. Jason Mason
647. Spooner
648. Rama of the Jungle
649. Lester Polyester
650. Mr. Moustache

a. Death of an Unpopular Poet
b. Miss You So Badly
c. It's Midnight, I'm Not Famous Yet
d. Incommunicado
e. Pencil Thin Mustache
f. Gypsies in the Palace
g. We Learned to be Cool from You
h. Elvis Presley Blues
i. Boat Drinks
j. That's What Living is to Me
k. Another Saturday Night
l. None

Answers are on the next page . . .

ANSWERS:

641. f: Snake/Gypsies in the Palace

642. d: Liberty Valance/Incommunicado

643. h: John Henry/Elvis Presley Blues

644. k: Frankenstein/Another Saturday Night

645. b: Zorro/Miss You So Badly

646. j: Jason Mason/That's What Living is to Me

647. a: Spooner/Death of an Unpopular Poet

648. e: Rama of the Jungle/Pencil Thin Mustache

649. c: Lester Polyester/It's Midnight, I'm Not Famous Yet

650. g: Mr. Moustache/We Learned to be Cool from You

Things to Know by Chart:

SAN FRANCISCO, CALIFORNIA
Latitude: 37° N
Longitude: 122° W

DIS & DAT / NUMBER 39:

651. Whose recognition do you seek in Mobile?

652. With whom did you stay up all night on your first date?

653. With what should you stay upstairs alone?

654. What did you seek in Biloxi?

655. After all that he had accomplished, what did the old man in Capt. Tony's say of the future?

656. How do people in the city pass the time?

657. Where are you going for Labor Day weekend?

658. How many pounds are involved in fat cat style?

659. What language is heard in the barbecue line?

660. What career might you have pursued had you not learned to sing?

Answers are on the next page . . .

Answers:

651. DJ/SAX

652. The blonde stranger/WTBS

653. The Good Book/TNART

654. Fortune and fame/YNWIDBA

655. There's still so much to be done/LMIP

656. Shooting one another/TC

657. San Francisco/CM

658. Three hundred/HDO

659. Hindu/BRSB

660. Merchant Marine/MIG

 Things to Know by Chart:

BOSTON, MASSACHUSETTS
Latitude: 42° N
Longitude: 71° W

Dis & Dat / Number 40:

661.   What is the reputation of the woman sitting with you?

662.   What did the sugar barons screw up?

663.   Who always said there is no free ride?

664.   What did your grandfather warn you about Brazil?

665.   If you laugh, joke, cuss, and smoke, what else are you likely to do?

666.   What three tiny things will your wings allow you to look down upon?

667.   Where was the neon sign flashing: "Jimmy Buffett, there's a great day a-comin'"?

668.   What weapon did you use against sparrows?

669.   Whose job is it to be different from the rest?

670.   What business is scary?

Answers are on the next page . . .

ANSWERS:

661.   Snuff queen/WDWGDAS

662.   The 'glades/TBOSW

663.   Your father/CW

664.   You might never come back again/FL

665.   Drink wine/WTCIC

666.   Tiny cars, tiny swimmers, and tiny beach bars/WING

667.   In your brain/GOD

668.   Rubber-tipped arrows/LIJATS

669.   Yours (the performer)/IMJ

670.   Rock and roll/VMATHG

Things to Know by Chart:

COCONUT GROVE, FLORIDA
Latitude: 25° N
Longitude: 80° W

DON' CHU KNOW / NUMBER 21:

Correctly match the number of the island with the letter of the song in which it is mentioned. To score correctly, you may use a song title only once.

671. Cedar Key   a. Migration

672. T'ree Mile Island   b. Mañana

673. Montserrat   c. Presents to Send You

674. Martinique   d. Volcano

675. Cayo Hueso   e. Desdemona's Building a Rocket Ship

676. Barbados   f. Six-string Music

677. Puerto Rico   g. Fins

678. St. Thomas   h. Meet Me in Memphis

679. Zanzibar   i. Everybody's Got a Cousin in Miami

680. Ramrod Key   j. I Have Found Me a Home

     k. Incommunicado

     l. None

Answers are on the next page . . .

ANSWERS:

671. k: Cedar Key/Incommunicado

672. d: T'ree Mile Island/Volcano

673. g: Montserrat/Fins

674. a: Martinique/Migration

675. i: Cayo Hueso/Everybody's Got a Cousin in Miami

676. c: Barbados/Presents to Send You

677. e: Puerto Rico/Desdemona's Building a Rocket Ship

678. b: St. Thomas/Mañana

679. f: Zanzibar/Six-string Music

680. h: Ramrod Key/Meet Me in Memphis

 Things to Know by Chart:

FANTASYLAND, FLORIDA
Latitude: 28° N
Longitude: 81° W

Dis & Dat / Number 41:

681.   Where might you find out who did dis & dat?

682.   Whom does the Queen of Sheba meet?

683.   What kind of dog does your lady have?

684.   Who could sound like the stars?

685.   What is it that the Remittance Man looks for?

686.   On what road did you pick up a hitchhiker from Nashville?

687.   Whose job is it to worry half to death?

688.   What did you do on the bar in Spago's?

689.   What is your cousin who lives in a coconut tree?

690.   What ended the performance of the Bob Roberts Society Band?

Answers are on the next page . . .

ANSWERS:

681. The Coconut Telegraph/COTE

682. He didn't attack/YNWIDBA

683. The Duke of Earl/WOTW

684. Billy Voltaire/CCOP

685. Absolution/RM

686. Highway 4/WNGBG

687. Your uncle, the self-made millionaire/IMJ

688. Puked/YNWIDBA

689. A Caribbean amphibian/CARAMPH

690. A blown circuit breaker/BRSB

Things to Know by Chart:

DALLAS, TEXAS
Latitude: 32° N
Longitude: 96° W

DIS & DAT / NUMBER 42:

691. What buries the past of Dafuskie Island?

692. What do you have hidden in your heart?

693. What is it that made you feel like a missing link?

694. What does your old lady bitch about?

695. Where does Norman say a thousand steps will lead?

696. What is it that warps the minds of city people?

697. How far did you go the first time that you ran?

698. What is it that Murphey, Walker, and Willis sing?

699. Before you leave for the Keys, what must you first do?

700. Who gave the railroad lady a fur and a diamond ring?

Answers are on the next page . . .

ANSWERS:

691. Bulldozers/POT

692. Some Texas/MIG

693. Hoodlum drink/FL

694. The mosquitoes/TWIHIWYWB

695. To nowhere/ATSTN

696. Proximity/ITC

697. End of the block/EOTR

698. Texas rhymes/MIG

699. Pay your bills/MLL

700. Some loner/RL

 Things to Know by Chart:

NEPAL, ASIA
Latitude: 28° N
Longitude: 84° E

OFF THE RECORD / NUMBER 4:

Live by the Bay was the first complete concert ever released on video by Jimmy. Filmed at Miami's Marine Stadium in 1985, Jimmy and the band were just then becoming accustomed to the phenomenon that only recently had been dubbed "Parrot Heads."

OTR 41. Who introduces Jimmy and the band to the stage?

OTR 42. In this version of Margaritaville, what does Jimmy sing is covered with oil"?

OTR 43. Whom does Jimmy introduce in the audience as "part of my problem?"

OTR 44. What song does Jimmy sing before interrupting himself with the comment "just kidding"?

OTR 45. What substance fills his waterbed?

OTR 46. What was written while Jimmy was trying to decide whether "to write a hit or commit suicide?"

OTR 47. What does Jimmy encourage Parrot Heads to do?

OTR 48. Which song has been "transformed into a video" about "marital infidelity"?

OTR 49. What does Jimmy drink before the encore?

OTR 50. How does he describe Mr. Utley's wardrobe?

Answers are on the next page . . .

ANSWERS:

Otr 41. Don Johnson, who was then riding high as Sonny Crockett on NBC's Miami Vice.

Otr 42. Turkeys/MAR

Otr 43. Captain Tony

Otr 44. Sailing (by Christopher Cross)

Otr 45. Crazy Glue/WDWGDAS

Otr 46. Come Monday/CM

Otr 47. He says he wants to see them squawk and flap their wings.

Otr 48. Who's the Blonde Stranger/WTBS

Otr 49. A bottle of Corona beer

Otr 50. Jimmy calls them pajamas.

INDECISIONS / NUMBER 7:

As clever and memorable as the titles of Jimmy's albums and songs might be, not every album includes a song with the same title. So, correctly label whether each of the following albums does have a title song (YES) or does not (NO) based only upon the information provided in the recorded lyrics.

701. YES/NO: Down to Earth

702. YES/NO: Hot Water

703. YES/NO: Riddles in the Sand

704. YES/NO: Living and Dying in ¾ Time

705. YES/NO: Barometer Soup

706. YES/NO: Floridays

707. YES/NO: Take the Weather with You

708. YES/NO: Somewhere Over China

709. YES/NO: A White Sport Coat and A Pink Crustacean

710. YES/NO: A1A

Answers are on the next page . . .

ANSWERS:

701. Down to Earth/NO

702. Hot Water/NO

703. Riddles in the Sand/NO

704. Living and Dying in ¾ Time/NO

705. Barometer Soup/YES

706. Floridays/YES

707. Take the Weather with You/NO
[Note: This is a trick question. The song on this album that carries the refrain of this album title is called simply "Weather With You."]

708. Somewhere Over China/YES

709. A White Sport Coat and A Pink Crustacean/NO

710. A1A/NO

 Things to Know by Chart:

TAHITI, SOCIETY ISLANDS
Latitude: 17° S
Longitude: 149° W

DON' CHU KNOW / NUMBER 22:

Correctly match the number of the religious reference with the letter of the song in which it is mentioned. To score correctly, you may use a song title only once.

711. St. Ignatius   a. Merry Christmas, Alabama

712. Sister Mary Mojo   b. Far Side of the World

713. Jesuit priest   c. Bank of Bad Habits

714. Guardian angels   d. The Missionary

715. Pharisees   e. The Ballad of Skip Wiley

716. Ramadan   f. That's My Story and I'm Stickin' to It

717. Altar boys   g. Spending Money

718. Gridiron madonna   h. Surfing in a Hurricane

719. St. Barbara   i. We are the People Our Parents Warned Us About

720. St. Christopher   j. Trouble on the Horizon

      k. Fruitcakes

      l. None

Answers are on the next page . . .

ANSWERS:

711.　c:　St. Ignatius/Bank of Bad Habits

712.　f:　Sister Mary Mojo/That's My Story and I'm Stickin' to It

713.　i:　Jesuit Priest/We are the People Our Parents Warned Us About

714.　a:　Guardian Angels/Merry Christmas, Alabama

715.　g:　Pharisees/Spending Money

716.　b:　Ramadan/Far Side of the World

717.　k:　Altar boys/Fruitcakes

718.　e:　Gridiron madonna/The Ballad of Skip Wiley

719.　j:　St. Barbara /Trouble on the Horizon

720.　h:　St. Christopher/Surfing in a Hurricane

 Things to Know by Chart:

NEW ORLEANS, LOUISIANA
Latitude: 30° N
Longitude: 90° W

Dis & DAT / NUMBER 43:

721. If you really do love the now, what unusual feat might the moon achieve?

722. If the moon is not at fault, then name one other thing that a temporary Frenchman might blame?

723. How many demerits are being piled up?

724. What three songs do have the word "moon" in their titles?

725. Beneath which moon does the Remittance Man confess?

726. In putting up a good fight, what piece of plumbing might as well be on the moon?

727. Who is the best friend of young Mr. Moon?

728. Who fell asleep on the beach beneath the Florida moon?

729. What type of flower is mentioned with the moonlight in your Alabama dream?

730. What do you see silhouetted by moonlight?

Answers are on the next page . . .

ANSWERS:

721. The moon jumps over the cow/ILTN

722. The Champs Élysées, a tune, or the stroke of Monet/FFTN

723. Beaucoup/AB

724. Everlasting Moon; Come to the Moon; Beach House on the Moon

725. The Bora Bora moon/RM

726. A shower stall/TGF

727. Magnus/CPLPE

728. Frank and Lola/FAL

729. Magnolia/SFOA

730. The island/ISL

 Things to Know by Chart:

LOS ANGELES, CALIFORNIA
Latitude: 34° N
Longitude: 118° W

DIS & DAT / NUMBER 44:

731.   Who would pay a tourist fare to sit on the bus with you?

732.   When you opened your window what had been written?

733.   What two dances do Carmen and Cugie perform?

734.   Where might you find your cojones in a hurricane?

735.   How late did you sleep during hurricane season?

736.   How did you feel sitting atop the mainmast?

737.   What might you get for a fin?

738.   What nickname do you tell Sinatra is not yours?

739.   What have you seen that was built by Howard Hughes?

740.   In cubic terms, how just how big is the diamond?

Answers are on the next page . . .

ANSWERS:

731. God/GDOAC(NW)

732. Your name/MS

733. Rhumba; boogie/TDDLCNM

734. In your throat!/SIAH

735. Past noon/TTRWHS

736. Half-assed/PB

737. A full tank/IHIWIT

738. Jack/MTK

739. Spaceship/TOTH

740. Cubic mile/DABATR

Things to Know by Chart:

MIAMI, FLORIDA
Latitude: 25° N
Longitude: 80° W

DON' CHU KNOW / NUMBER 23:

Correctly match the number of the alcoholic beverage with the letter of the song in which it is mentioned. To score correctly, you may use a song title only once.

741.	Singapore Sling	a.	Altered Boy
742.	Daiquiri	b.	Landfall
743.	Scotch	c.	Blue Guitar
744.	Rose	d.	The Weather is Here, I Wish You Were Beautiful
745.	Gin	e.	Brahma Fear
746.	Tequila	f.	Margaritaville
747.	Pouilly Frusse	g.	Duke's On Sunday
748.	Whiskey	h.	It's Five O'Clock Somewhere
749.	Red Wine	i.	You Call It Joggin'
750.	Hurricane	j.	Semi-True Story
		k.	Big Rig
		l.	None

Answers are on the next page . . .

ANSWERS:

741. a: Singapore Sling/Altered Boy

742. d: Daiquiri/The Weather is Here, I Wish You
            Were Beautiful

743. k: Scotch/Big Rig

744. g: Rose/Duke's On Sunday

745. i: Gin/You Call It Joggin'

746. j: Tequila/Semi-True Story

747. b: Pouilly Frusse/Landfall

748. e: Whiskey/Brahma Fear

749. c: Red wine/Blue Guitar

750. h: Hurricane/It's Five O'Clock Somewhere

 Things to Know by Chart:

ST. MARTIN, WEST INDIES
Latitude: 18° N
Longitude: 63° W

DIS & DAT / NUMBER 45:

751. How does the girl with the ballpark figure try to keep her boyfriend slim?

752. What two presents do you get on Christmas?

753. In what state did you stare at the guitar in a museum?

754. What occupation was written on the sign you carried into the first row?

755. What smell do you associate with the house of your aunt and uncle?

756. What can you barely control?

757. In what state did you fall asleep at the wheel?

758. What sight assured you that you had survived your car accident?

759. How much money was spent just to get a look at Mars?

760. What surrounds an altered boy?

Answers are on the next page . . .

ANSWERS:

751. She hides his cookies when he gets the munchies/CLI

752. Jam and wax/UOTHT

753. Tennessee/SWCT

754. Baker ("I need the dough")/DNT

755. The creosote plant/LIJATS

756. Your Caribbean soul/MIG

757. Illinois/LIJATS

758. A tire swing hanging from a tree/LIJATS

759. Ninety jillion dollars/FRU

760. Fun/AB

Things to Know by Chart:

MARQUESAS ISLANDS, PACIFIC OCEAN
Latitude: 9° S
Longitude: 140° W

DIS & DAT / NUMBER 46:

761. What piece of furniture have you just bought?

762. What fruits are on Carmen's headwear?

763. What can your lady eat in the Keys?

764. What mountain do you say they named well?

765. What sort of storm gives no warning?

766. Who is it that you can talk to when the coast is clear?

767. Where do they say it is supposed to get better?

768. What does Kinja lack?

769. What did you drink once you were lowered from the mainmast?

770. What instrument did he learn to play after he went to Paris?

Answers are on the next page . . .

ANSWERS:

761. Waterbed/WDWGDAS

762. Bananas; mangoes/TDDLCNM

763. Crabmeat/MLL

764. Crazy Mountain/RD

765. Gravity storm/GS

766. Yourself/WTCIC

767. Cane Garden Bay/MAN

768. Water/TLONP

769. Perrier/PB

770. Piano/HWTP

Things to Know by Chart:

BUTLER TOWN, JAMAICA
Latitude: 18° N
Longitude: 77° W

Don' chu know / number 24:

Correctly match the number of the holiday with the letter of the song in which it is mentioned. To score correctly, you may use a song title only once.

771.	Labor Day	a.	The Night I Painted the Sky
772.	Halloween	b.	Changes in Latitudes, Changes in Attitudes
773.	Bastille Day	c.	Chansons Pour Les Petit Enfants
774.	Carnival	d.	High Cumberland Jubilee/Comin' Down
775.	Easter	e.	Frenchman for the Night
776.	Mardi Gras	f.	When Salome Plays the Drum
777.	Christmas	g.	Desperation Samba
778.	Independence Day	h.	Lone Palm
779.	Jubilee	i.	Barefoot Children in the Rain
780.	Judgment Day	j.	Life is just a Tire Swing
		k.	Come Monday
		l.	None

Answers are on the next page . . .

ANSWERS:

771. k: Labor Day/Come Monday

772. g: Halloween/Desperation Samba (Halloween in Tijuana)

773. e: Bastille Day/Frenchman for the Night

774. f: Carnival/When Salome Plays the Drum

775. j: Easter/Life is Just a Tire Swing

776. l: Mardi Gras/None

777. h: Christmas/Lone Palm

778. a: Independence Day/The Night I Painted the Sky

779. d: Jubilee/High Cumberland Jubilee

780. i: Judgment Day/Barefoot Children in the Rain

Things to Know by Chart:

CAROLINE STREET, KEY WEST, FLORIDA
Latitude: 24° N
Longitude: 82° W

DIS & DAT / NUMBER 47:

781. What will you be pushing-up in the old boneyard?

782. Who is a Vulcan in disguise?

783. What was Nordstrom's plan intended to save?

784. With what did the brand new country star replace his old guitar?

785. Which of John Wayne's films are you thinking of?

786. Where are we all, sooner or later?

787. What advice do you not want to be told?

788. What sight gives you a lump in your throat?

789. What wardrobe would you buy for your trip to Martinique?

790. What do you know of the bank in Ringling?

Answers are on the next page . . .

ANSWERS:

781. Daisies/OVK

782. Cameron/BHOTM

783. His ass/LAN

784. A Japanese electric guitar/BNCS

785. Red River; (The Man Who Shot) Liberty Valance/INC

786. In the stew/CAL

787. To get Rolfed/WATPOPWUA

788. A flying boat/SIW

789. A Bogart suit/MIG

790. It's been torn down/RR

 Things to Know by Chart:

ARUBA, ANTILLES
Latitude: 12° N
Longitude: 70° W

DIS & DAT / NUMBER 48:

791. How many years of beer cans have piled up in Ringling?

792. What sort of food might you eat in the Himalayas?

793. What part of the body is considered to be just a muscle?

794. What does Santa ride in the Caribbean?

795. Who was looking for Melissa?

796. What does every night wear?

797. Who inherited the unpopular poet's royalties?

798. Where have the kids gone once the superslide has closed?

799. What nearly ran over Frank and Lola?

800. What did the railroad lady do with her diamond ring?

Answers are on the next page . . .

ANSWERS:

791. Twenty-seven/RR

792. Milky Ways/OVK

793. Heart/SS

794. A dolphin/CITC

795. Ricardo/COTE

796. A new disguise/LVD

797. His dog, Spooner/DOAUP

798. Back to school/WTCIC

799. The lifeguard's Jeep/FAL

800. Pawned it/RL

Things to Know by Chart:

BILOXI, MISSISSIPPI
Latitude: 30° N
Longitude: 88° W

INDECISIONS / NUMBER 8:

Jimmy sings at least 15 songs that mention the names of actual cities or towns in the title. So, correctly mark each of the following as being part of a song title (TRUE) or not part of a song title (FALSE), based upon Jimmy's recorded lyrics.

801. TRUE/FALSE: Biloxi

802. TRUE/FALSE: Dallas

803. TRUE/FALSE: Denver

804. TRUE/FALSE: New York

805. TRUE/FALSE: Livingston

806. TRUE/FALSE: London

807. TRUE/FALSE: Louisville

808. TRUE/FALSE: Memphis

809. TRUE/FALSE: Savannah

810. TRUE/FALSE: Tijuana

Answers are on the next page . . .

ANSWERS:

801. Biloxi: TRUE/BIL

802. Dallas: TRUE/DAL

803. Denver: TRUE/AMHID

804. New York/FALSE

805. Livingston: TRUE/LSN

806. London/FALSE

807. Louisville/FALSE

808. Memphis: TRUE/MMIM

809. Savannah: TRUE

810. Tijuana: TRUE/DS/HIT

DON' CHU KNOW / NUMBER 25:

Correctly match the number of the food item with the letter of the song in which it is mentioned. To score correctly, you may use a song title only once.

811. Fried chicken   a. I Wish Lunch Could Last Forever

812. Deviled egg   b. Creola

813. Coconut tart   c. Landfall

814. Chowder   d. Life is just a Tire Swing

815. Snapper fried light   e. Far Side of the World

816. Doughnuts   f. Honey Do

817. Sardines   g. Death of an Unpopular Poet

818. Steak and bacon   h. Livingston Saturday Night

819. Sticky bun   i. Blue Heaven Rendezvous

820. Gumbo   j. The Wino and I Know

                             k. What If the Hokey Pokey is All It
                                 Really is About

                             l. None

Answers are on the next page . . .

ANSWERS:

811.   d: Fried chicken/Life is Just a Tire Swing

812.   h: Deviled egg/Livingston Saturday Night

813.   a: Coconut tart/I Wish Lunch Could Last Forever

814.   f: Chowder/Honey Do

815.   c: Snapper fried light/Landfall

816.   j: Doughnuts/The Wino and I Know

817.   e: Sardines/Far Side of the World

818.   g: Steak and bacon/Death of an Unpopular Poet

819.   k: Sticky bun/What If the Hokey Pokey is All It Really is About

820.   b: Gumbo/Creola

Things to Know by Chart:

SAN JUAN AIRPORT, PUERTO RICO
Latitude: 18° N
Longitude: 66° W

DIS & DAT / NUMBER 49:

821. What should an expatriated American first learn?

822. What is the name of Carmen's dance partner?

823. What challenging situation might your son provide?

824. What do you follow past bamboo shacks?

825. What do the men in Porto Bello quack about?

826. Who made you think you might want to stay in Tampico?

827. What word best described the unpopular poet after his death?

828. Where might one now find the Chicamauga?

829. What is Desdemona's passion?

830. Who is it that you talk to when the coast is clear?

Answers are on the next page . . .

ANSWERS:

821. Some native customs/BARE

822. Cugie (Xavier Cugat)/TDDLCNM

823. Trying on a dress/SCO

824. Songlines/FSOTW

825. Fishing/CITJ

826. The women/TT

827. Immortal/DOUAP

828. At the bottom of Mobile Bay/FE

829. Cookies/DBARS

830. Yourself/WTCIC

 Things to Know by Chart:

WEST NASHVILLE, TENNESSEE
Latitude: 36° N
Longitude: 86° W

DIS & DAT / NUMBER 50:

831. What time do the landsharks feed?

832. What is there no time to count?

833. How long did you shoot the breeze in Capt. Tony's?

834. What has been your condition now for over two weeks?

835. If you're not yet famous, what time might it be?

836. What video game might you play on a Saturday night?

837. If you live through Thursday, what will happen on Friday?

838. What has nature put upon a Capricorn and Taurus?

839. When did young Mr. Moon and his friend leave the island?

840. When did the semi-normal person say that he'd be home?

Answers are on the next page . . .

ANSWERS:

831. Right after dark/FINS

832. What you're worth/VOL

833. For hours/LMIP

834. You've been drunk/APLAF

835. Midnight/IMINFY

836. Pong/LSN

837. You'll be roarin'/MHH

838. Handcuffs/ICBYHT

839. Sunrise/CPLPE

840. When he got back/SOC

Things to Know by Chart:

MELBOURNE, FLORIDA
Latitude: 38° N
Longitude: 80° W

Don' chu know / number 26:

Correctly match the number of the fictional character with the letter of the song in which it is mentioned. To score correctly, you may use a song title only once.

841. Flying Dutchman

842. Captain Kangaroo

843. Boston Blackie

844. Mr. Clean

845. Melissa

846. HAL

847. Billy Clyde

848. Merita

849. Travis McGee

850. Peter Pan

a. Cuban Crime of Passion

b. Captain America

c. Fruitcakes

d. Take It Back

e. Incommunicado

f. Ho, Ho, Ho and a Bottle of Rhum

g. Coconut Telegraph

h. Ballad of Skip Wiley

i. Remittance Man

j. The Weather is Here, I Wish You Were Beautiful

k. Pencil Thin Mustache

l. None

Answers are on the next page . . .

ANSWERS:

841. i: Flying Dutchman/Remittance Man

842. d: Captain Kangaroo/Take It Back

843. k: Boston Blackie/Pencil Thin Mustache

844. b: Mr. Clean/Captain America

845. g: Melissa/Coconut Telegraph

846. c: HAL/Fruitcakes

847. j: Billy Clyde/The Weather is Here, I Wish You Were Beautiful

848. a: Merita/Cuban Crime of Passion

849. e: Travis McGee/Incommunicado

850. f: Peter Pan/Ho,Ho,Ho and a Bottle of Rhum

Things to Know by Chart:

HOLLYWOOD, CALIFORNIA
Latitude: 34° N
Longitude: 118° W

DIS & DAT / NUMBER 51:

851. Whose music do you listen to as you walk along the beach?

852. What letter could you not master in penmanship?

853. What is the main squeeze in the backseat?

854. In what city did Billy meet Merita?

855. Where did you spend a year of your life one night?

856. What challenging situation might your son provide?

857. Where do you see a gold wedding band?

858. What might a lucky person get in Livingston?

859. Other than California, what else wears you thin?

860. What word might best describe high school honeys?

Answers are on the next page . . .

Answers:

851. Bob Marley's/FRU

852. Small L/TVM

853. Accordion/USSZ

854. Havana/CCOP

855. Beirut/FLO

856. Trying on your daughter's dress/SCO

857. On a trembling hand/WTWLBM

858. Laid!/LAN

859. Bimbo limbo/SWIARSS

860. Fickle/DRE

 Things to Know by Chart:

AUSTIN, TEXAS
Latitude: 30° N
Longitude: 97° W

DIS & DAT / NUMBER 52:

861. Where might one find an advertisement for Domino College?

862. What would happen if we couldn't laugh?

863. How much do you earn working in a dive?

864. If you had eight legs, what would you call your brain?

865. What are you doing when you hear your leg snap?

866. What does Little Miss Magic love about riding through town?

867. What did the neighborhood murderer raise?

868. Where does your girlfriend run off with your car?

869. What did the bush doctor make them swear?

870. What are you going to get in Leadville?

Answers are on the next page . . .

ANSWERS:

861. In a matchbook (in a hotel room)/DC

862. We'd all go insane/CIL,CIA

863. Twenty-six dollars/PBC

864. Pea brain/DBM

865. Rounding first base/GOBNU

866. Feeling the breeze/LMM

867. Hamsters/VMATHG

868. To her ma and pa/SA

869. Not to tell/CPLPE

870. Beer/INC

 Things to Know by Chart:

PORT AU PRINCE, HAITI
Latitude: 18° N
Longitude: 72° W

DON' CHU KNOW / NUMBER 27:

Correctly match the number of the food item with the letter of the song in which it is mentioned. To score correctly, you may use a song title only once.

871.	Hot dogs	a.	Kinja Rules
872.	Mulligan Stew	b.	Dreamsicle
873.	Bouillabaisse	c.	The Legend of Norman Paperman/ Kinja
874.	Enchilada	d.	Spending Money
875.	Popcorn	e.	Frank and Lola
876.	Country Ham	f.	Dixie Diner
877.	Apple pie	g.	Lage Nom Ai
878.	Crabmeat	h.	Please Bypass This Heart
879.	Turkey	i.	Captain America
880.	Olives	j.	What If the Hokey Pokey is All It Really is About
		k.	My Lovely Lady
		l.	None

Answers are on the next page . . .

ANSWERS:

871. c: Hot dogs/The Legend of Norman Paperman

872. f: Mulligan stew/Dixie Diner

873. g: Bouillabaisse/Lage Nom Ai

874. a: Enchilada/Kinja Rules

875. e: Popcorn/Frank and Lola

876. b: Country Ham/Dreamsicle

877. i: Apple pie/Captain America

878. k: Crabmeat/My Lovely Lady

879. d: Turkey/Spending Money

880. j: Olives/What If the Hokey Pokey is All It Really is About

 Things to Know by Chart:

DECATUR, ALABAMA
Latitude: 33° N
Longitude: 84° W

DIS & DAT / NUMBER 53:

881. What instrument is played by the person who went into a blues rampage?

882. What does Steve Martin want?

883. Where did the semi-normal person go?

884. Where might one find Old Man Rhythm?

885. Whose halitosis could vaporize cars?

886. Who rode in a ragtop from South Beach to Key West?

887. What was it that your co-conspirator was responsible for watching in the Mini-Mart?

888. What is in your leg?

889. How much do you plan to pay your agent?

890. What could have been your title in kindergarten?

Answers are on the next page . . .

ANSWERS:

881. Harmonica/FB

882. To get small/MAN

883. The Orient/SOC

884. In your shoes/SC

885. Godzilla's/OTSTL

886. Bella rode while Lenny drove/CONT

887. The big, round mirror/PBC

888. A pin/INC

889. 15% of nothing = nothing/YNWITBA

890. King of Excuses/TMSAISTI

 Things to Know by Chart:

ORLANDO, FLORIDA
Latitude: 28° N
Longitude: 81° W

DIS & DAT / NUMBER 54:

891. What sort of people have bad hair and pimples?

892. What is it that you are ready to do?

893. Who would say grace at the Sunday table?

894. What have you been doing for nearly half a century?

895. What color is your ragtop?

896. By what star did the Jolly Mon find his way?

897. How do old men wearing tank tops spend their time?

898. How are the holes in your heart and in the ocean alike?

899. What aircraft would you love to drive?

900. What might someone buy if he wins the football pool?

Answers are on the next page . . .

ANSWERS:

891. Television preachers/FRU

892. Anything, anytime, anywhere/AAA

893. Auntie Mae/CRE

894. Singing in a band/OTWT

895. White and red/RTD

896. Orion/JMS

897. Cruising by gift shops/MAR

898. Both are big and blue/BL

899. The shuttle/SOC

900. Some grass/DRE

Things to Know by Chart:

SAN DIEGO, CALIFORNIA
Latitude: 32° N
Longitude: 117° W

O
F
F

T
H
E

R
E
C
O
R
D

Off the Record / Number 5:

So, here is one last page about videos on the enhanced tracks of music CDs, as well as on the DVDs: MiniMatinee #1, Live in Hawaii, Live at Fenway Park, Live at Wrigley Field, Scenes You Know by Heart, and Live in Anguilla.

OTR 51.   What is the venue for the Anguilla concert?

OTR 52.   What four-letter word is emblazoned across the front of Jimmy's shirt in the Hey Good Lookin' video?

OTR 53.   Who introduces the Live at Wrigley Field DVD?

OTR 54.   To whom do Jimmy and Mac play a musical tribute from the bleacher seats?

OTR 55.   What does Ralph McDonald play for percussion in Knees of My Heart?

OTR 56.   What song does Jimmy sing in an Airstream trailer?

OTR 57.   What is the only song that Jimmy is shown performing in Key West?

OTR 58.   What is Jimmy's dressing room complaint on the enhanced video track for Tuesdays, Thursdays, Saturdays?

OTR 59.   What horn does Jimmy play on the Don't Stop the Carnival enhanced track?

OTR 60.   By what mode of transportation does Jimmy arrive at Fenway Park?

Answers are on the next page . . .

ANSWERS:

OTR 51. The Dune Preserve Bar & Restaurant owned by Bankie Banx/LIVE IN ANGUILLA

OTR 52. HANK [Williams]/HGL

OTR 53. Ernie Banks/LIVE AT WRIGLEY FIELD

OTR 54. Steve Goodman/LIVE AT WRIGLEY FIELD

OTR 55. First, two sheets of paper; then, two plastic bags/KOMH

OTR 56. Far Side of the World/FSOTW

OTR 57. We Are the People on the stage of Margaritaville/
WATPOPWUA

OTR 58. The shower head is aimed directly toward the door of the shower stall itself, so he bitches about the water.

OTR 59. Trombone

OTR 60. Duckboat/LIVE AT FENWAY PARK

INDECISIONS / NUMBER 9:

Aside from the obvious A Pirate Looks at Forty, Jimmy has recorded a few other songs that mention pirates. So, correctly label each of the following song titles either PIRATE or NONE based only upon the information provided in the recorded lyrics.

901. PIRATE/NONE: Champagne Sí, Agua No

902. PIRATE/NONE: Love in the Library

903. PIRATE/NONE: Migration

904. PIRATE/NONE: Ballad of Skip Wiley

905. PIRATE/NONE: Off to See the Lizard

906. PIRATE/NONE: Last Mango in Paris

907. PIRATE/NONE: Jolly Mon Sing

908. PIRATE/NONE: Everybody's Got a Cousin in Miami

909. PIRATE/NONE: Son of a Son of a Sailor

910. PIRATE/NONE: A Salty Piece of Land

Answers are on the next page . . .

ANSWERS:

901. Champagne Sí, Agua No/PIRATE

902. Love in the Library/PIRATE

903. Migration/NONE

904. Ballad of Skip Wiley/PIRATE

905. Off to See the Lizard/PIRATE

906. Last Mango in Paris/NONE

907. Jolly Mon Sing/PIRATE

908. Everybody's Got a Cousin in Miami/PIRATE

909. Son of a Son of a Sailor/NONE

910. A Salty Piece of Land/PIRATE

 Things to Know by Chart:

ST. AUGUSTINE, FLORIDA
Latitude: 29° N
Longitude: 81° W

Don' chu know / number 28:

Every now and then during a song, Jimmy will address the band or a specific band member. Correctly match the number of such a remark with the letter of the song in which it is mentioned. To score correctly, you may use a song title only once.

911. Mr. Utley!

912. Take it, Marvin!

913. Let's reggae, Reefers!

914. Let's stir it up, boys!

915. All right, blues torpdoes!

916. Let's take a lap.

917. Thank you, Robot!

918. Mister T . . .

919. Harpoon Man!

920. Take us to church, Sonny

a. Coastal Confessions

b. Hey Good Lookin'

c. Fool Button

d. Stars Fell on Alabama

e. They Don't Dance Like Carmen No More

f. Honey Do

g. Volcano

h. Mañana

i. You Call It Joggin'

j. Everybody's Got A Cousin in Miami

k. None

Answers are on the next page . . .

ANSWERS:

911. g: Mr. Utley!/Volcano

912. e: Take it, Marvin!/They Don't Dance Like Carmen No More

913. g: Let's reggae, Reefers!/Mañana

914. b: Let's stir it up, boys!/Hey Good Lookin'

915. f: All right, blues torpedoes!/Honey Do

916. i: Let's take a lap!/You Call It Joggin'

917. j: Thank you, Robot!/Everybody's Got A Cousin in Miami
      [Note: Actually, Jimmy is addressing Robert Greenidge, but he pronounces the name with a Caribbean lilt and accent. Thus, "Robert" comes out as "Robot."]

918. d: Mister T . . . /Stars Fell on Alabama

919. c: Harpoon Man!/Fool Button

920. a: Take us to church, Sonny/Coastal Confessions

Things to Know by Chart:

BOURBON STREET, NEW ORLEANS, LOUISIANA
Latitude: 30° N
Longitude: 90° W

DIS & DAT / NUMBER 55:

921. Who has mentioned "the landing gear?"

922. Where does Ace sleep at night?

923. Who is Stanley Kubrick's buddy?

924. What are you using to fight inflation?

925. If it is time to change the subject, what sort of beverage would you offer?

926. What is the other job of your agent?

927. What might you have done beneath your school desk in the '50s?

928. What cliché describes the body of the girl who was banned from the Chart Room?

929. What did you wear in the first row (of Let's Make A Deal)?

930. What happened to your hair the last time you drank tequila?

Answers are on the next page . . .

ANSWERS:

921. The engineer/NPOS

922. On a bench/ACE

923. HAL/FRU

924. Quarters in your loafers/WATPOPWUA

925. Herbal tea/WITHPIAIRIA

926. Bondsman/YNWIDBA

927. Kissed your ass goodbye/WFTNE

928. Ballpark figure/CLI

929. A beer barrel/DNT

930. Had it pulled out/PTSY

 Things to Know by Chart:

BISCAYNE BAY, FLORIDA
Latitude: 25° N
Longitude: 80° W

DIS & DAT / NUMBER 56:

931. What drifts by without any names?

932. What do you ask your honey to throw over the rail?

933. If you were the last man standing, what would you be holding in your hand?

934. How does the purple people eater get around?

935. What can become of a blessing kept to yourself?

936. What sort of license do you hold?

937. What must be bought by anyone losing at dominoes?

938. Where does the night wind take you?

939. What sort of hat did you buy on a shopping spree?

940. What is on the corner of Government and Bay Avenue?

Answers are on the next page . . .

ANSWERS:

931. Days/IHFMAH

932. The compass/OASTBC

933. A fun ticket/LMS

934. Flying/PPE

935. A curse/DABATR

936. To fly/SBH

937. Booze/DC

938. Just where you want/LVD

939. Antique/LS

940. Doomsday fanatic/LITL

 Things to Know by Chart:

CHAMPS ÉLYSÉES, PARIS, FRANCE
Latitude: 48° N
Longitude: 2° E

DON' CHU KNOW / NUMBER 29:

Correctly match the number of the landmark with the letter of the song in which it is mentioned. To score correctly, you may use a song title only once.

941. Orange Bowl   a. Everybody's Got A Cousin in Miami

942. South Station   b. Volcano

943. Duvalier Airport   c. Somewhere Over China

944. Madison Avenue   d. Morris' Nightmare

945. Comanche Skypark   e. African Friend

946. Sea World   f. Migration

947. Fantasyland   g. Pencil Thin Mustache

948. Great Wall   h. Frenchman for the Night

949. Grove Drugstore   i. Railroad Lady

950. Disneyland   j. Baby's Gone Shopping

     k. The Ballad of Skip Wiley

     l. None

Answers are on the next page . . .

Answers:

941. k: Orange Bowl/The Ballad of Skip Wiley

942. i: South Station/Railroad Lady

943. e: Duvalier Airport/African Friend

944. j: Madison Avenue/Baby's Gone Shopping

945. b: Comanche Skypark/Volcano

946. d: Sea World/Morris' Nightmare

947. f: Fantasyland/Migration

948. c: Great Wall/Somewhere Over China

949. a: Grove Drugstore/Everybody's Got A Cousin in Miami

950. g: Disneyland/Pencil Thin Mustache

Things to Know by Chart:

MONTGOMERY, ALABAMA
Latitude: 32° N
Longitude: 86° W

DIS & DAT / NUMBER 57:

951. What can you do to a flock of pink flamingos?

952. Where might you find Binky and Bunny?

953. What was job of Jesus' father?

954. With what do you want your back scratched?

955. Where did you pass out during hurricane season?

956. What does the genius never asked for?

957. Who just passed you in that station wagon full of kids?

958. What is the smell from your jogging honey's wet hair?

959. What kind of fame do you not want?

960. What do the Jamaicans promise if you return?

Answers are on the next page . . .

ANSWERS:

951. Pray/TOTH

952. Up on the hill/UOTH

953. Chopping sugar cane/HDA

954. Lightning bolt/BCITH

955. Hammock/TTRWHS

956. Promises/AHAG

957. Your baby's husband/RTD

958. Shampoo, instead of sweat/YCIJ

959. The kind that brings confusion (like being recognized on a plane)/MLL

960. Not to shoot you out of the sky/JM

Things to Know by Chart:

RAMROD KEY, FLORIDA
Latitude: 25° N
Longitude: 82° W

DIS & DAT / NUMBER 58:

961. What latitude does the Remittance Man follow?

962. From disorder, what direction do you travel?

963. For what port is Tiki bound?

964. If you are off Miami in a boatload of suntan oil with a rental goat, where might you be headed?

965. What island is located in a windward archipelago?

966. What sort of people sing and shout in Paraguay?

967. In what region had you spent all the money you'd saved?

968. Where did you get the money to burn in Las Vegas?

969. Where has Livingston gone?

970. Where does the sun shine daily on the mountain top?

Answers are on the next page . . .

Answers:

961. The equator/RM

962. Southeast/SOASOAS

963. Shanghai/WATPOPWUA

964. Domino College/DC

965. Kinja/TLONP

966. Gauchos/CITJ

967. Coast of Marseilles/COM

968. A big tax return/CTCED

969. Texas/LGTT

970. Jamaica/JF

 Things to Know by Chart:

MERIDIAN, MISSISSIPPI
Latitude: 32° N
Longitude: 88° W

Don' chu know / number 30:

Correctly match the number of the celestial body with the letter of the song in which it is mentioned. To score correctly, you may use a song title only once.

971. Moon	a. That's My Story, and I'm Sticking to It
972. Mars	b. Cowboy in the Jungle
973. Earth	c. Everybody's Got a Cousin in Miami
974. Pleiades	d. Whoop De Doo
975. Southern Cross	e. California Promises
976. Venus	f. Desdemona's Building a Rocket Ship
977. Jupiter	g. Volcano
978. Satellite	h. Chanson Pours Les Petits Enfants
979. Quasar	i. Jolly Mon Sing
980. Orion	j. Jimmy Dreams
	k. Flesh and Bone
	l. None

Answers are on the next page . . .

ANSWERS:

971. d: Moon/Whoop De Doo

972. a: Mars/That's My Story

973. g: Earth/Volcano

974. j: Pleiades/Jimmy Dreams

975. b: Southern Cross/Cowboy in the Jungle

976. h: Venus/Flesh and Bone

977. l: Jupiter/Chanson Pours Les Petits Enfants

978. c: Satellite/Everybody's Got a Cousin in Miami

979. f: Quasar/Desdemona's Building A Rocket Ship

980. i: Orion/Jolly Mon Sing

Things to Know by Chart:

BUZIOS, BRAZIL
Latitude: 22° S
Longitude: 43° W

DIS & DAT / NUMBER 59:

981.   How many years has Spider John been on the road?

982.   What does Groovy tell the waitress about his chicken?

983.   What must you do to make it out in Hollywood?

984.   From what island does the lady hail?

985.   What is the contraband that you can't take with you?

986.   What is it that amazes Little Miss Magic?

987.   What prevented you from getting to Bridgetown?

988.   What does a cultural infidel do in the dark?

989.   Who is the environmental terrorist?

990.   Where will you take your pony?

Answers are on the next page . . .

Answers:

981. Thirty/BOSJ

982. It had died in vain/COC

983. Change and complain/YNWIDBA

984. Trinidad (island of the spices)/SOASOAS

985. Money/CW

986. Blades of the ceiling fan/LMM

987. You had smoked a whole lid/PTSY

988. Paint/CI

989. Skip Wiley/TBOSW

990. To the shore/TAR

 Things to Know by Chart:

RED RIVER, TEXAS
Latitude: 34° N
Longitude: 99° W

Dis & DAT / NUMBER 60:

991. What is the home state of the railroad lady?

992. What did the band think of the person who was on a blues rampage?

993. Aside from dope, what other two things are in short supply?

994. On what island was Norman Paperman born?

995. Where had your African friend just concluded his business?

996. What can you juggle?

997. What have you seen to make the world spin?

998. What sort of people could survive on beer and bread?

999. What sort of people might you encounter on the bus?

1000. What indicates that a gypsy song is coming on?

Answers are on the next page . . .

ANSWERS:

991. Kentucky/RL

992. He's a jerk/FB

993. Women; water/MAN

994. Manhattan/PR

995. Aruba/AF

996. Verbs, adverbs, and nouns/IIAFD

997. Enough/OPH

998. Old time sailors/CIP

999. Half-baked/FRU

1000. Red sky at dawn/BBTM

Things to Know by Chart:

MARGARITAVILLE, FLORIDA
Latitude: 24° N
Longitude: 82° W

THE ESSAY QUESTION:

Okay, you've had it pretty easy 'til now; however, the moment for cleansing your brain has arrived at last. If you believe that you can answer the following question in 500 words or less, then feel free to send your essay to me, in care of the publisher (whose address is in the front part of this book). Include some way that I might contact you in return. Otherwise, good luck.

1001. Why don't we get drunk and screw?

Don't even bother looking on the next page for your answer. I'm outta here!

219

SONG CODES

AAA	Anything, Anytime, Anywhere (License to Chill)
AAOG	An Attitude of Gratitude (Thanks & Giving All Year Long)
AATH	Ass and the Hole (Word of Mouth)
AB	Altered Boy (Far Side of the World)
ABNM	A Brand New Me (The Now Generation: Hits Are Our Business)
ACE	Ace (High Cumberland Jubilee/Before the Salt/Before the Beach/Collector's Edition: There's Nothing Soft About Hard Times/Best of the Early Years(Legend)/There's Nothing Soft/Captain America/Down to Earth-High Cumberland/Now Yer Squawkin')
ADR	Autour du Rocher (Far Side of the World/Live in Anguilla/v)
AF	African Friend (Son of a Son of a Sailor/Boats, Beaches, Bars & Ballads/Club Trini Margaritaville Café Late Night Gumbo/A Pirate's Treasure)
AHAG	Ain't He a Genius (Down to Earth/Jimmy Buffett/Before the Salt/American Storyteller Collector's Edition: There's Nothing Soft About Hard Times/Best of the Early Years (Legend)/There's Nothing Soft About Hard Times/Captain America/Singers, Songwriters, and Legends/Down to Earth-High Cumberland Jubilee/Now Yer Squawkin')
AIWFC	All I Want for Christmas is My Two Front Teeth ('Tis the SeaSon)
ALTDA	A Lot to Drink About (Buffet Hotel)
AMELIT	All My Ex's Live in Texas (Live at Texas Stadium)
AMHID	A Mile High in Denver (Down to Earth/Jimmy Buffett/Before the Salt/Before the Beach/ American Storyteller/Collector's Edition: There's Nothing Soft About Hard Times/Best of the Early Years(Legend)/There's Nothing Soft About Hard Times/ Captain America/Singers, Songwriters, and Legends/Down to Earth-High Cumberland Jubilee/Now Yer Squawkin')
ANL	All Night Long (Tuskegee)
AOT	Abandoned on Tuesday (Audio Mobile single)
APLAF	A Pirate Looks at Forty (A1A/You Had to Be There/ Songs You Know by Heart/ Live by the Bay/Feeding Frenzy/Boats, Beaches, Bars & Ballads/Biloxi/All the Great Hits/A Pirate's Treasure/Tuesdays, Thursdays, Saturdays/Meet Me in Margaritaville/Live in: Auburn /Vegas/Mansfield/Cincinnati/Hawaii/Live at Fenway Park/Live at Wrigley Field/Live in Anguilla/Scenes You Know by Heart/Encores)
APO	Apocalypso (Fruitcakes/Live in Mansfield)
ASC	A Sailor's Christmas (Christmas Island)
ASN	Another Saturday Night (Margaritaville Café Late Night Menu)
ASPOL	A Salty Piece of Land (A Salty Piece of Land CD)
ATSTN	A Thousand Steps to Nowhere (Don't Stop the Carnival)
ATWIWY	All the Ways I Want You (Far Side of the World)
BAL	Bend a Little (High Cumberland Jubilee/Before the Salt/Before the Beach/Collector's Edition: There's Nothing Soft About Hard Times/ Best of the Early Years (Delta & Legend)/ Captain America/Down to Earth-High Cumberland/Now Yer Squawkin')
BAMA	Bama Breeze (Take the Weather With You)
BARE	Banana Republics (Changes in Latitudes, Changes in Attitudes/All the Great Hits/Live at Wrigley Field/v/Encores)
BB	Barstool Boogie (Selected Shorts)
BBOH	Bluebird of Happiness (Audio Mobile single)
BBTM	Bring Back the Magic (Hot Water)
BCITR	Barefoot Children in the Rain (Barometer Soup/Meet Me in Margaritaville)
BD	Boat Drinks (Volcano/Songs You Know by Heart/Boats, Beaches, Bars & Ballads/All the Great Hits/Live in Hawaii/Live at Fenway Park/v/Scenes You Know by Heart/v)

BEG	Brown-Eyed Girl (One Particular Harbour/Boats, Beaches, Bars & Ballads/Tuesdays, Thursdays, Saturdays/Great American Summer Fun/Meet Me in Margaritaville/Live in Las Vegas/Live at Fenway/Live at Wrigley Field/Live in Anguilla
BF	Brahma Fear (Living and Dying in ¾ Time)
BFTN	Barefootin' (Hoot Soundtrack)
BG	Blue Guitar (Far Side of the World)
BGS	Baby's Gone Shopping (Hot Water)
BH	Buffet Hotel (Buffet Hotel)
BHOTM	Beach House on the Moon (Beach House on the Moon, Bonus track video)
BHR	Blue Heaven Rendezvous (Barometer Soup)
BIBOMO	Breathe In, Breathe Out, Move On (Take the Weather With You)
BICO	Baby, It's Cold Outside [feat. Nadirah Shakoor] ('Tis the SeaSon)
BIL	Biloxi (Changes in Latitudes, Changes in Attitudes/Biloxi)
BIRI	Big Rig (Havana Daydreamin')
BITW	Blowin' in the Wind (Encores)
BL	Boomerang Love (Off to See the Lizard/Always Soundtrack/Live in Cincinnati)
BNCS	Brand New Country Star (Living and Dying in ¾ Time/Biloxi)
BOBH	Bank of Bad Habits (Barometer Soup/Great American Summer Fun)
BOSJ	Ballad of Spider John (Living and Dying in ¾ Time/Boats, Beaches, Bars & Ballads)
BRSB	Bob Roberts Society Band (Banana Wind/Meet Me in Margaritaville)
BS	Barometer Soup (Barometer Soup)
BSW	Beautiful Swimmers (Buffet Hotel)
BT	Big Top (Buffet Hotel)
BTB	Burn that Bridge (Riddles in the Sand/Live in Auburn/Live in Cincinnati)
BTE	Beyond the End (Last Mango in Paris/Live in Hawaii)
BTOB	Boats to Build (License to Chill/Live at Texas Stadium)
BTTBOU	Bigger than the Both of Us (Riddles in the Sand)
BTTI	Back to the Island (License to Chill/Live in Hawaii)
BW	Banana Wind (Banana Wind)
CA	Captain America (Down to Earth/Jimmy Buffett/Before the Salt/Before the Beach/American Storyteller/Collector's Edition:There's Nothing Soft About Hard Times/Best of the Early Years (Legend) /There's Nothing Soft About Hard Times/Captain America/Singers, Songwriters, and Legends/Down to Earth-High Cumberland/Now Yer Squawkin')
CAL	Calaloo (Don't Stop the Carnival)
CARAMPH	Caribbean Amphibian (Elmopalooza Soundtrack)
CC	Changing Channels (Off to See the Lizard/Boats, Beaches, Bars & Ballads)
CCOP	Cuban Crime of Passion (A White Sport Coat and A Pink Crustacean/Boats, Beaches, Bars & Ballads/Live at Fenway Park/v)
CDMIM	Cinco de Mayo in Memphis (Take the Weather With You)
CHD	Cumberland High Dilemma (High Cumberland Jubilee/Before the Salt/Jimmy Buffett/Before the Beach/Collector's Edition: There's Nothing Soft About Hard Times/Best of the Early Years(Delta & Legend)/Captain America/Now Yer Squawkin')
CHR	The Christian? (Down to Earth/Before the Salt/American Storyteller/Collector's Edition: There's Nothing Soft About Hard Times/Best of the Early Years (Legend)/There's Nothing Soft/Captain America/Down to Earth-High Cumberland Jubilee/Now Yer Squawkin')
CHRISL	Christmas Island (Christmas Island, Elton John's Christmas Party)
CI	Cultural Infidel (Banana Wind)
CIL,CIA	Changes in Latitudes, Changes in Attitudes (Changes in Latitudes, Changes in Attitudes/You Had to Be There/Songs You Know by Heart/Live by the Bay/Feeding Frenzy/Boats, Beaches, Bars & Ballads/Great American Summer Fun/Biloxi/All the Great Hits/A Pirate's Treasure/Meet Me in Margaritaville/Live in Auburn/Live in Las Vegas/Live in Mansfield/Live in Cincinnati/Live in Hawaii, Live at Fenway Park/Live at Wrigley Field/v/Live in Anguilla/v/Scenes You Know by Heart/v)
CIP	Cheeseburger in Paradise (Son of a Son of a Sailor/Songs You Know by Heart/Live bythe Bay/ Feeding Frenzy/Boats, Beaches, Bars & Ballads/The Parakeet Album/Great American Summer Fun/Biloxi/All the Great Hits/Tuesdays, Thursdays, Saturdays/ Meet Me in Margaritaville/ Live in Auburn/ Live in Las Vegas/Live in Mansfield /Live in Cincinnati/Live in Hawaii/Live at Fenway Park / Live at Wrigley Field Live in Anguilla/Scenes You Know by Heart)

SONG CODES

S O N G   C O D E S

CITC	Christmas in the Caribbean (Tennessee Christmas/The Parakeet Album/Boats, Beaches, Bars & Ballads)
CITJ	Cowboy in the Jungle (Son of a Son of a Sailor/Meet Me in Margaritaville)
CLI	Clichés (Havana Daydreamin')
CM	Come Monday (Living and Dying in ¾ Time/You Had to Be There/*Coast to Coast* Soundtrack /Songs You Know by Heart/Live by the Bay/ Feeding Frenzy/Boats, Beaches, Bars & Ballads/ Great American Summer Fun/All the Great Hits/A Pirate's Treasure/Tuesdays, Thursdays, Saturdays/ Meet Me in Margaritaville/Live in Auburn/Live in Las Vegas/Live in Mansfield/Live in Cincinnati/Live in Hawaii)/Live at Fenway Park/Live at Wrigley Field/Live in Anguilla/Scenes You Know by Heart/Encores)
COAC	Coastal Confession (License to Chill)
COC	Coast of Carolina (License to Chill/Live at Fenway Park/v/Encores)
COM	Coast of Marseilles (Son of a Son of a Sailor/Boats, Beaches, Bars & Ballads/A Pirate's Treasure/Encores)
CONO	City of New Orleans (Live at Wrigley Field/v)
CONT	Conky Tonkin' (License to Chill)
COTE	Coconut Telegraph (Coconut Telegraph/Live by the Bay/Biloxi/Tuesdays, Thursdays, Saturdays /Meet Me in Margaritaville/Live in Mansfield/Live in Hawaii)
COTW	Champion of the World (Join the Band)
CP	California Promises (One Particular Harbour/Boats, Beaches, Bars & Ballads/Biloxi)
CPLPE	Chanson Pour Les Petits Enfants (Volcano/All the Great Hits/The Parakeet Album/Live in Anguilla/v)
CRE	Creola (Floridays/Meet Me in Margaritaville/Nod to the Storyteller)
CRWIS	Can't Remember When I Slept Last (*Rancho Deluxe* Soundtrack)
CS,AN	Champagne Sí, Agua No (Don't Stop the Carnival)
CT	Cattle Truckin' (*Rancho Deluxe* Soundtrack)
CTCED	Countin' the Cows Every Day (*Rancho Deluxe* Soundtrack)
CTOG	Come Together (The Now Generation: Come Together)
CTTM	Come to the Moon (Riddles in the Sand/The Parakeet Album)
CW	Carnival World (Off to See the Lizard/Live in Anguilla/v)
DABATR	Diamond as Big as the Ritz (Barometer Soup)
DAL	Dallas (A1A)
DBARS	Desdemona's Building A Rocket Ship (Banana Wind)
DBM	Don't Bug Me (*Arachnophobia* Soundtrack)
DC	Domino College (Boats, Beaches, Bars & Ballads/Live in Anguilla/v)
DCK	Don' Chu Know (Barometer Soup)
DD	Dixie Diner (You Had to Be There)
DG	Defying Gravity (Havana Daydreamin'/Boats, Beaches, Bars & Ballads/Live at Fenway Park/v/Encores)
DIL	Distantly in Love (One Particular Harbour/Boats, Beaches, Bars, Ballads/Live Anguilla)
DNT	Door Number Three (A1A/Live by the Bay)
DOAUP	Death of An Unpopular Poet (A White Sport Coat and A Pink Crustacean/Encores)
DOM	Domicile (Don't Stop the Carnival)
DOS	Duke's On Sunday (Take the Weather With You)
DOTC	Down On The Corner (The Now Generation: Hits Are Our Business)
DRE	Dreamsicle (Volcano)
DS/HIT	Desperation Samba (Halloween in Tijuana) (Last Mango in Paris/Boats, Beaches, Bars & Ballads/Meet Me in Margaritaville/Live in Anguilla/v)
DTP	Drivin' the Pig (Manejando el Cerdo) ('Tis the SeaSon)
DTTS	Delaney Talks to Statues (Fruitcakes/The Parakeet Album)
DVL	Death Valley Lives (High Cumberland Jubilee/Before the Salt/Before the Beach/Collector's Edition: There's Nothing Soft About Hard Times/Best of the Early Years(Legend)/There's Nothing Soft About Hard Times/Captain America/Down to Earth-High Cumberland/ Now Yer Squawkin'/Down to Earth-High Cumberland/Now Yer Squawkin')
DYKWIM	Do You Know What It Means to Miss New Orleans (Encores)
ED	Ellis Dee (Down to Earth/Jimmy Buffett/Before the Salt/Before the Beach/American Storyteller/Collector's Edition: There's Nothing Soft/Best of the Early Years (Legend)/ There's Nothing Soft/Captain America/Down to Earth-High Cumberland/Now Yer Squawkin')
EGACIM	Everybody's Got a Cousin in Miami (Fruitcakes)

EI	Elvis Imitators (Boats, Beaches, Bars & Ballads)
EM	Everlasting Moon (Boats, Beaches, Bars & Ballads)
ENG	England (High Cumberland Jubilee/Before the Salt/Before the Beach/Down to Earth-High Cumberland/Now Yer Squawkin')
EOTP	Everybody's on the Phone (Take the Weather With You)
EOTR	Everybody's on the Run (Last Mango in Paris)
EPB	Elvis Presley Blues (Take the Weather With You)
ET	Everybody's Talkin' (Meet Me in Margaritaville/Live in Auburn/Live in Las Vegas/Live in Mansfield/Live in Cincinnati/Live in Hawaii)
FAB	Flesh and Bone (Beach House on the Moon/Forever Tams)
FAL	Frank and Lola (Last Mango in Paris/Boats, Beaches, Bars & Ballads)
FB	Fool Button (Son of a Son of a Sailor)
FD	Funeral Dance (Don't Stop the Carnival)
FE	False Echoes (Banana Wind)
FFTN	Frenchman for the Night (Fruitcakes/Nod to the Storyteller)
FG	Fifteen Gears (*Rancho Deluxe* Soundtrack)
FINS	Fins (Volcano/Songs You Know by Heart/Live by the Bay/Feeding Frenzy/Boats, Beaches, Bars & Ballads/Biloxi/All the Great Hits/Tuesdays, Thursdays, Saturdays/Today Presents/Meet Me in Margaritaville/Live in Auburn/Live in Las Vegas/Live in Mansfield/Live in Cincinnati/Live in Hawaii/Live at Fenway Park/Live at Wrigley Field/v/Live in Anguilla/v/Scenes You Know by Heart/v)
FL	First Look (Floridays/Boats, Beaches, Bars & Ballads)
FLO	Floridays (Floridays, *Hoot* Soundtrack)
FPM	Fat Person Man (Don't Stop the Carnival)
FRU	Fruitcakes (Fruitcakes/Great American Summer Fun/Tuesdays, Thursdays, Saturdays/Tales from MargaritaVision/Meet Me in Margaritaville/Live at Fenway Park/v)
FSOTW	Far Side of the World (Far Side of the World(v)/Live in: Auburn/Hawaii)
GCG	Go Cubs Go (Live at Wrigley Field/v)
GCH	Gulf Coast Highway (Evangeline)
GDOAC/NW	God Don't Own a Car (No Wheels)(High Cumberland Jubilee/Before the Salt/Before the Beach/American Storyteller/Collector's Edition: There's Nothing Soft About Hard Times/Best of the Early Years(Legend)/There's Nothing Soft About Hard Times/Captain America/Singers, Songwriters, and Legends/ Down to Earth-High Cumberland/Now Yer Squawkin')
GFAS	Green Flash at Sunset (Don't Stop the Carnival unlisted track/video)
GF/JF	Grapefruit-Juicy Fruit (A White Sport Coat and A Pink Crustacean/You Had toBe There/Songs You Know by Heart/Live by the Bay/Boats, Beaches, Bars & Ballads/Biloxi/All the Great Hits/A Pirate's Treasure/Meet Me in Margaritaville/Live in Auburn/Live in Hawaii/Live at Fenway Park/Live in Anguilla/v/Scenes You Know by Heart/v)
GFSH	Great Filling Station Holdup (A White Sport Coat and A Pink Crustacean/Boats, Beaches, Bars & Ballads/Biloxi/Live at Fenway Park)
GH	Great Heart (Hot Water/Live in Auburn/Live in Las Vegas/Live in Mansfield/Live in Cincinnati/Live in Hawaii/v)
GITP	Gypsies in the Palace (Last Mango in Paris/Feeding Frenzy/Live in Auburn/Live in Las Vegas/Live in Mansfield/Live in Cincinnati/Live in Hawaii/Live at Fenway Park)
GOBNU	Growing Older But Not Up (Coconut Telegraph/Meet Me in Margaritaville/Live in Cincinnati/Encores)
GOD	God's Own Drunk (Living and Dying in ¾ Time/You Had to Be There)
GRO	Groovin' (The Now Generation: Hits Are Our Business)
GS	Gravity Storm (Off to See the Lizard/Live in Las Vegas/Live in Mansfield)
GGW	Good Guys Win (*Hoot* Soundtrack)
GTP	Getting the Picture (*Sports Illustrated* 2007 Swimsuit Edition bonus video)
HCJ/CDS	High Cumberland Jubilee/Comin' Down Slow (High Cumberland Jubilee/Before the Salt/Before the Beach/Collector's Edition: There's Nothing Soft About Hard Times/Best of the Early Years (Delta & Legend)/Captain America/Singers,Songwriters,and Legends/Down to Earth-High Cumberland/Now Yer Squawkin')
HDA	Havana Daydreamin' (Havana Daydreamin'/You Had to Be There/Boats, Beaches, Bars & Ballads/Biloxi/Meet Me in Margaritaville)
HDO	Honey Do (One Particular Harbour/Songs You Know by Heart/Feeding Frenzy/Live in Mansfield/Live in Cincinnati)

HEANT	Happily Ever After (Now and Then) (Banana Wind)
HEY	Hey Jude (Music for Montserrat)
HGAH	Hula Girl at Heart (Take the Weather With You)
HGL	Hey Good Lookin' (License to Chill/v/Live at Fenway Park/Live at Wrigley Field/v/Live at Texas Stadium/Scenes You Know by Heart/v)
HHHA	Ho, Ho, Ho and A Bottle of Rhum (Christmas Island)
HH:QM	Hippolyte's Habitat (Qui Moun' Qui) (Don't Stop the Carnival)
HM	Homemade Music (Hot Water/Tales from MargaritaVision)
HOL	Holiday (Banana Wind/Meet Me in Margaritaville)
HOM	Howlin' Moon (From the Reach)
HS:TK	Henny's Song: The Key to My Man (Don't Stop the Carnival)
HT	Hello Texas (Urban Cowboy Soundtrack)
HTW	Honky Tonk Women (The Now Generation: Hits Are Our Business)
HWA	Here We Are (Take the Weather With You/Enhanced CD track)
HWTP	He Went to Paris (A White Sport Coat and A Pink Crustacean/You Had to Be There/Songs You Know by Heart/Boats, Beaches, Bars & Ballads/All the Great Hits/A Pirate's Treasure/Tales from MargaritaVision/Meet Me in Margaritaville/Scenes You Know by Heart/v/Encores)
HX/WI	Happy Xmas/War is Over (Christmas Island)
IAATW	It's All About the Water (Don't Stop the Carnival)
IABOG	It's A Big Old Goofy World (Encores)
IBHFC	I'll be Home for Christmas (Christmas Island)
ICBYH	I Can't be Your Hero Today (Down to Earth/Jimmy Buffett/Before the Salt/Before the Beach/American Storyteller/Collector's Edition: There's Nothing Soft About Hard Times/Best of the Early Years (Legend)/ There's Nothing Soft About Hard Times/Captain America/Singers, Songwriters, and Legends/ Down to Earth-High Cumberland/Now Yer Squawkin')
IDK	I Don't Know (Spicoli's Theme) (*Fast Times at Ridgemont High* Soundtrack/Live in Auburn/Live in Las Vegas)
IDKAIDC	I Don't Know and I Don't Care (Beach House on the Moon)
IF	Island Fever (Don't Stop the Carnival)
IFOS	It's Five O'clock Somewhere (Alan Jackson: Greatest Hits 2/Mini Matinee 1/Live in Auburn/Live in Las Vegas/Live in Mansfield/Live in Cincinnati/Live in Hawaii/Live at Fenway Park/Live at Wrigley Field/v/Live at Texas Stadium/Live in Anguilla/v/Scenes You Know by Heart/v/Alan Jackson: 34 Number Ones)
IHFMAH	I Have Found Me A Home (A White Sport Coat and A Pink Crustacean/Boats, Beaches, Bars & Ballads)
IHIWIT	I Heard I was in Town (Somewhere Over China/Boats, Beaches, Bars & Ballads)
IIAFD	If It All Falls Down (Floridays)
IICJGIOP	If I Could Just Get It on Paper (Somewhere Over China)
ILTN	I Love The Now (Floridays)
IMBH	It Must Be Him (The Now Generation: Hits Are Our Business)
IMINFY	It's Midnight, I'm Not Famous Yet (Somewhere Over China/Live in Las Vegas)
IMJ	It's My Job (Coconut Telegraph/Live in Auburn/Live in Mansfield/Live in Cincinnati/Live in Hawaii)
IMR	In My Room (Live in Anguilla/v)
INC	Incommunicado (Coconut Telegraph/Boats, Beaches, Bars & Ballads)
ISL	Island (Coconut Telegraph/Boats, Beaches, Bars & Ballads)
ISMS	I Still Miss Someone (Live in Auburn)
ITPDR	If the Phone Doesn't Ring It's Me (Last Mango in Paris/Live by the Bay/Boats, Beaches, Bars & Ballads)
ITS	In the Shelter (Before the Beach/Changes in Latitudes, Changes in Attitudes/Beach Music Anthology/ Collector's Edition: There's Nothing Soft About Hard Times/Best of the Early Years (Legend)/There's Nothing Soft About Hard Times/Captain America/Meet Me in Margaritaville/Live in Auburn/Live in Las Vegas/Live in Mansfield/Live in Cincinnati/Live in Hawaii/Down to Earth-High Cumberland/Now Yer Squawkin')
IUTHM	I Use to Have Money One Time (One Particular Harbour)
IWLCLF	I Wish Lunch Could Last Forever (Off to See the Lizard)
IWPFG	I Will Play for Gumbo (Beach House on the Moon/Live at Wrigley Field/v)
JAOTT	Just An Old Truth Teller (Don't Stop the Carnival)

JB	Jingle Bells (Christmas Island/Now That's What I Call Christmas!)
JBR	Jingle Bell Rock ('Tis the SeaSon)
JD	Jimmy Dreams (Barometer Soup)
JEAN	Jean (The Now Generation: Come Together)
JF	Jamaica Farewell (Feeding Frenzy/Tales from MargaritaVision)
JM	Jamaica Mistaica (Banana Wind)
JMS	Jolly Mon Sing (Last Mango in Paris/Feeding Frenzy/Boats, Beaches, Bars & Ballads/A Pirate's Treasure/Meet Me in Margaritaville/Live in Las Vegas/Live in Hawaii/Live at Fenway Park/v)
KD	Knee Deep (You Get What You Give/v)
KIISW	Kick it in Second Wind (Havana Daydreamin'/Boats, Beaches, Bars & Ballads)
KOMH	Knees of My Heart (Riddles In the Sand/Boats, Beaches, Bars & Ballads/Meet Me in Margaritaville/Live in Auburn/Live in Mansfield/Live in Cincinnati)
KOSH	King of Somewhere Hot (Hot Water/Live in Anguilla/v)
KR	Kinja Rules (Don't Stop the Carnival)
LAL	Love and Luck (Boats, Beaches, Bars & Ballads/Tuesdays, Thursdays, Saturdays)
LAN	Lage Nom Ai (Barometer Soup)
LBOS	Little Bit of Soul (The Now Generation: Come Together)
LC	Lovely Cruise (Changes in Latitudes, Changes in Attitudes/Boats, Beaches, Bars & Ballads/Live in Las Vegas/Live in Mansfield/Encores)
LDLL	L'air de la Louisianne (Hot Water/Encores)
LF	Landfall (Changes in Latitudes, Changes in Attitudes/You Had to Be There)
LGTT	Livingston's Gone to Texas (High Cumberland Jubilee/Living and Dying in ¾ Time/Before the Salt/Before the Beach/American Storyteller/Collector's Edition: There's Nothing Soft About Hard Times/Best of the Early Years (Legend)/There's Nothing Soft About Hard Times/Captain America/Singers, Songwriters, and Legends/Down to Earth-High Cumberland/Now Yer Squawkin')
LICE	Lady I Can't Explain (Volcano)
LID	Love in Decline (Riddles in the Sand)
LIJATS	Life is Just a Tire Swing (A1A)
LIU	Livin' It Up (One Particular Harbour/Tales from MargaritaVision)
LITL	Love in the Library (Fruitcakes)
LMIP	Last Mango in Paris (Last Mango in Paris/Live by the Bay/Feeding Frenzy/Biloxi/All the Great Hits/Tuesdays, Thursdays, Saturdays/Meet Me in Margaritaville/Live at Wrigley Field/Encores)
LMM	Little Miss Magic (Coconut Telegraph/Boats, Beaches, Bars, Ballads/The Parakeet Album/A Pirate's Treasure)
LMS	Last Man Standing (Far Side of the World)
LMWANTD	Left Me with a Nail to Drive (*Rancho Deluxe* Soundtrack)
LOAJP	Leaving On A Jet Plane (The Now Generation: Come Together)
LP	Lone Palm (Fruitcakes)
LS	Lip Service (Somewhere Over China)
LSCN	Life Short, Call Now (Buffet Hotel)
LSN	Livingston Saturday Night (*Rancho Deluxe* Soundtrack/Son of a Son of a Sailor/*FM* Soundtrack/Boats, Beaches, Bars & Ballads/Biloxi/A Pirate's Treasure)
LTC	License to Chill (License to Chill, *Sports Illustrated* 2004 Swimsuit CD/v/Live at Fenway Park/v/Live at Wrigley Field/v)
LTTC	Last Train to Clarksville (The Now Generation: Come Together)
LUCST	Lucky Stars (Beach House on the Moon)
LVD	La Vie Dansante (Riddles in the Sand/The Parakeet Album/Tales from MargaritaVision/Live at Wrigley Field/Nod to the Storyteller)
MAN	Mañana (Son of a Son of a Sailor/Boats, Beaches, Bars, Ballads/Biloxi/A Pirate's Treasure)
MAR	Margaritaville (Changes in Latitudes, Changes in Attitudes/You Had to Be There/Songs You Know by Heart/Live by the Bay/Feeding Frenzy/Boats, Beaches, Bars & Ballads/Biloxi/All the Great Hits/A Pirate's Treasure/Tuesdays, Thursdays, Saturdays/Under the Influence/Meet Me in Margaritaville/*Anger Management* Soundtrack/Live in Mansfield/Live in Las Vegas/Live in Mansfield/Live in Cincinnati/Live in Hawaii/Legends: We Will Rock You/Live at Fenway Park/Lotta Love Concert/Live at Wrigley Field/v/ Live at Texas Stadium/Live in Anguilla/v/Scenes You Know by Heart/iTunes single w/Bret Michaels)
MASU	Math Suks (Beach House on the Moon)

S O N G C O D E S

MB	My Barracuda (Hot Water)
MBG	Money Back Guarantee (Boats, Beaches, Bars & Ballads)
MCA/N	Merry Christmas, Alabama/Never Far from Home (Christmas Island)
MEX	Mexico (Barometer Soup/Live in Auburn/Live in Las Vegas/Live in Mansfield/Live in Cincinnati/Live in Hawaii)
MF	Mental Floss (Banana Wind)
MHH	My Head Hurts, My Feet Stink, and I Don't Love Jesus (Havana Daydreamin')
MICH	Michelle (The Now Generation: Hits Are Our Business)
MIG	Migration (A1A/Meet Me in Margaritaville)
MK	Mele Kalikimaka (Christmas Island/'Tis the SeaSon [feat. Jake Shimabukuro])
MLL	My Lovely Lady (A White Sport Coat and A Pink Crustacean)
MITN	Mermaid in the Night (Off to See the Lizard)
MMFM	Makin' Music For Money (A1A)
MMIM	Meet Me in Memphis (Floridays)
MN	Morris' Nightmare (You Had to Be There)
MOTN	Middle of the Night (Neville Brothers: Tell It Like It Is/v/Boats, Beaches, Bars & Ballads)
MS	Mr. Spaceman (Kermit the Frog – Unpigged)
MTK	Mack the Knife (Duets II with Frank Sinatra)
MVVD	Mademoiselle (Voulez Vous Danser) (Far Side of the World)
MYSB	Miss You So Badly (Changes in Latitudes, Changes in Attitudes/All the Great Hits)
MYBO	My Bonnie (The Now Generation: Come Together)
NBAB	Nothing But A Breeze (Take the Weather With You)
NFN	Nobody from Nowhere (Buffet Hotel)
NML	Never My Love (The Now Generation: Come Together)
NNHH	Na Na, Hey Hey Kiss Him Goodbye (The Now Generation: Hits Are Our Business)
NPOS	No Plane On Sunday (Floridays)
NSTTC	Nobody Speaks to the Captain No More (Floridays)
NTW	Northeast Texas Women (Live at Texas Stadium)
NW	Nautical Wheelers (A1A/Boats, Beaches, Bars & Ballads/A Pirate's Treasure/Tales from MargaritaVision/(Encores)
OAP	Oysters and Pearls (Beach House on the Moon/Encores)
OASBTC	On a Slow Boat to China (Somewhere Over China/Boats, Beaches, Bars & Ballads/A Pirate's Treasure)
OPH	One Particular Harbour (One Particular Harbour/Songs You Know by Heart/Live by the Bay/Feeding Frenzy/Boats, Beaches, Bars & Ballads/Great American Summer Fun/A Pirate's Treasure/Tuesdays, Thursdays, Saturdays/Tales from MargaritaVision/Meet Me in Margaritaville/Live in Auburn/Live in Las Vegas/Live in Mansfield/Live in Cincinnati/Live in Hawaii/Live at Fenway Park/Live at Wrigley Field/v/Live in Anguilla/v[two CD versions]
OPW	Oh, Pretty Woman (The Now Generation: Come Together)
OTSTL	Off to See the Lizard (Off to See the Lizard/The Parakeet Album)
OTWT	Only Time Will Tell (Banana Wind)
OVK	Overkill (Banana Wind)
OW	One World (Bridge to Havana)
PAP	Peddlers and Pushers
PAR	Paradise (Encores)
PASC	Pascagoula Run (Off to See the Lizard/Boats, Beaches, Bars & Ballads/Meet Me in Margaritaville /Live at Fenway Park/Live at Wrigley Field/v)
PATE	Party at the End of the World (Take the Weather With You)
PB	Perrier Blues (You Had to Be There)
PBC	Peanut Butter Conspiracy (A White Sport Coat and A Pink Crustacean)
PBTH	Please Bypass This Heart (Last Mango in Paris)
PD	Poopi Doo (Audio Mobile 45 rpm single)
PDBMC	Please Don't Bring Me Candy (Audio Mobile 45 rpm single)
POT	Prince of Tides (Hot Water)
POW	Piece of Work (License to Chill/Live at Fenway Park/Live at Wrigley Field/v)
PPE	Purple People Eater (Contact Soundtrack)
PR	Public Relations (Don't Stop the Carnival)
PR/R	Public Relations/Reprise (Don't Stop the Carnival)
PROATF	Permanent Reminder of a Temporary Feeling (Beach House on the Moon)

PTC	Pacing the Cage (Beach House on the Moon)
PTLA	Playin' the Loser Again (License to Chill)
PTM	Pencil Thin Mustache (Living and Dying in ¾ Time/You Had to Be There/ Songs You Know by Heart/Boats, Beaches, Bars & Ballads/All the Great Hits/ A Pirate's Treasure/Tuesdays,Thursdays,Saturdays/Tales from MargaritaVision/ Best of Toe the Line: Lindancers' Favourites/(Meet Me in Margaritaville/Live in Las Vegas/Live at Fenway Park/Scenes You Know by Heart/v)
PTSY	Presents to Send You (A1A)
PTYDFY	Please Take Your Drunken 15 Year-Old Girlfriend Home (Second Wind)
PY	Pre-You (Hot Water/Boats, Beaches, Bars & Ballads)
QMN	Quietly Making Noise (Fruitcakes)
QV	Quiet Village (Live in Hawaii)
RA	Reggae Accident (Margaritaville Café Late Night Menu)
RATCT	Rockin' Around the Christmas Tree ('Tis the SeaSon)
RD	Rancho Deluxe/Main & End Title (Rancho Deluxe Soundtrack)
RKF	Raindrops Keep Falling On My Head (The Now Generation: Hits Are Our Business
REDS	Redemption Song (Live in Anguilla)
RESP	Respect (Live at Fenway Park/v)
RF	Richard Frost (Down to Earth/Jimmy Buffett/Before the Salt/American Story-teller/Collector's Edition: There's Nothing Soft About Hard Times /Best of the Early Years (Legend)/There's Nothing Soft About Hard Times/Captain America/Now Yer Squawkin')
RH	Reggabilly Hill (Take the Weather With You/Encores)
RHM	Rhumba Man (Buffet Hotel)
RIS	Ridin' in Style (Rancho Deluxe Soundtrack)
RL	**Railroad Lady (A White Sport Coat and A Pink Crustacean)**
RM	Remittance Man (Barometer Soup)
RR	Ringling, Ringling (Living and Dying in ¾ Time)
RRR	Run, Rudolph, Run (Christmas Island)
RS	Rockefeller Square (High Cumberland Jubilee/Before the Salt/Before the Beach/Singers, Songwriters, and Legends/Down to Earth-High Cumberland/Now Yer Squawkin')
RTD	Ragtop Day (Riddles in the Sand/The Slugger's Wife Soundtrack/Live by the Bay/Boats, Beaches, Bars & Ballads)
RTRNR	Rudolph the Red-Nosed Reindeer ('Tis the SeaSon)
SA	Sunny Afternoon (Fruitcakes)
SAM	South America (Imagination)
SAX	Saxophones (Living and Dying in ¾ Time/Meet Me in Margaritaville/Live in Auburn/ Live in Mansfield/Live in Cincinnati)
SB	Strange Bird (Off to See the Lizard)
SBEG	Scarlet Begonias (License to Chill/Live at Fenway/v/Live at Wrigley Field/v)
SBH	School Boy Heart (Banana Wind/Meet Me in Margaritaville/Live in Las Vegas/Live in Mansfield/Live at Wrigley Field/v)
SC	Sea Cruise (Margaritaville Café New Orleans, Late Night Gumbo/Music for Our Mother Ocean, Vol. 3/Live in Mansfield)
SCA	Sweet Caroline (Live at Fenway Park/v)
SCO	Simply Complicated (License to Chill)
SCR	Southern Cross (Tuesdays, Thursdays, Saturdays/Live in Las Vegas/Live in Cincinnati/Live at Wrigley Field/v/Live in Anguilla/v)
SFOA	Stars Fell on Alabama (Coconut Telegraph/Songs for Sleepless Nights/All the Great Hits/A Pirate's Treasure)
SFYW	Savannah Fare You Well (Far Side of the World)
SGMH	Sure Gonna Miss Her (The Now Generation: Come Together)
SGOOMM	She's Going Out of My Mind (Riddles in the Sand)
SGRA	Some Gothic Ranch Action (Rancho Deluxe Soundtrack)
SGY	She's Got You (Fruitcakes)
STI	Still in Paradise (Live in Anguilla/v)
SIAH	Surfing in a Hurricane (Buffet Hotel)
SIUTK	Someone I Used to Know (License to Chill)
SIW	Someday I Will (Far Side of the World)
SM	Spending Money (Beach House on the Moon)

SONG CODES

SOAS	Stranded on a Sandbar (Volcano)
SOASOAS	Son of a Son of a Sailor (Son of a Son of a Sailor/You Had to Be There/Songs You Know by Heart/Boats, Beaches, Bars & Ballads/Biloxi/All the Great Hits/A Pirate's Treasure/Tuesdays, Thursdays, Saturdays/Meet Me in Margaritaville/*Hollywood's Magic Island: Catalina* Soundtrack/Live in Auburn/Live in Las Vegas/Live in Mansfield/Live in Cincinnati/Live in Hawaii/Live at Fenway Park/Live at Wrigley Field/Live in Anguilla/Nod to Storyteller/Scenes You Know by Heart)
SOC	Somewhere Over China (Somewhere Over China)
SOH	Sea of Heartbreak (License to Chill/Live at Texas Stadium)
SOS	Sail On Sailor (Meet Me in Margaritaville)
SOTW	Stars on the Water (One Particular Harbour/Live by the Bay/Boats, Beaches, Bars & Ballads/The Firm Soundtrack)
SOU	Souvenirs (Margaritaville Café Late Night Menu)
SS	Sheila Says (Don't Stop the Carnival)
SSFAA	Something So Feminine about a Mandolin (Havana Daydreamin')
SSM	Six-string Music (Fruitcakes)
SST	Santa Stole Thanksgiving ('Tis the SeaSon)
STE	Steamer (Somewhere Over China/Boats, Beaches, Bars & Ballads)
STS	Semi-True Story (Beach House on the Moon)
STOM	Sending the Old Man Home (Volcano/Boats, Beaches, Bars & Ballads)
SUG	Sugar Sugar (The Now Generation: Come Together)
SUM	Summerzcool (Buffet Hotel)
SUR	Survive (Volcano/*Coast to Coast* Soundtrack/Boats, Beaches, Bars & Ballads/Love Flashback Collection)
SUS	Suspicious Minds (The Now Generation: Come Together)
SWBT	Someday We'll Be Together (The Now Generation: Come Together)
SWCT	Stories We Could Tell (A1A/Live in Hawaii)
SW	Silver Wings (Take the Weather With You)
SWIAR	Smart Woman (in a Real Short Skirt) (Hot Water)
TA	Turning Around (*Summer Rental* Soundtrack)
TAATH	The Ass and the Hole (Word of Mouth)
TAB	Turnabout (High Cumberland Jubilee/Before the Salt/Before the Beach/Down to Earth-High Cumberland Jubilee/Now Yer Squawkin')
TAR	Take Another Road (Off to See the Lizard/Tales from MargaritaVision/Meet Me in Margaritaville)
TATS	Trip Around the Sun (License to Chill/v)
TBAMF	These Boots Are Made For Walkin' (The Now Generation: Hits Are Our Business)
TBIO	Tiki Bar is Open (Mini Matinee 1/Live in Auburn/Live in Las Vegas/Live in Mansfield/Live in Cincinnati/Live in Hawaii)
TBOSW	The Ballad of Skip Wiley (Barometer Soup)
TCATK	The Captain and the Kid (Down to Earth/Jimmy Buffett/Before the Salt/Before the Beach/Havana Daydreamin'/ Boats, Beaches, Bars & Ballads/American Storyteller/Collector's Edition: There's Nothing Soft About Hard Times /Best of the Early Years (Legend)/There's Nothing Soft About Hard Times/Captain America/Meet Me in Margaritaville/Down to Earth-High Cumberland/Now Yer Squawkin')
TC	The City (Feeding Frenzy/Tales from MargaritaVision//Live at Wrigley Field/v)
TCC	Tin Cup Chalice (A1A/Tuesdays, Thursdays, Saturdays/Meet Me in Margaritaville/Encores)
TDDLC	They Don't Dance Like Carmen No More (A White Sport Coat and a Pink Crustacean/Live in Anguilla/v)
TDOC	The Twelve Days of Christmas (Parrothead Version) ('Tis the SeaSon)
TF	Treetop Flyer (Banana Wind hidden track)
TGF	The Good Fight (Coconut Telegraph)
THFITC	The Handiest Frenchman in the Caribbean (Don't Stop the Carnival)
THOG	The Hang Out Gang (High Cumberland Jubilee/Before the Salt/Before the Beach/Collector's Edition: There's Nothing Soft About Hard Times/Best of the Early Years (Delta & Legend)/Captain America/Down to Earth-High Cumberland/Now Yer Squawkin')
THLAL	Treat Her Like A Lady (Volcano/Live in Anguilla/v)
THR	This Hotel Room (Havana Daydreamin'/Live in Las Vegas/Live in Cincinnati)
TIB	Take It Back (Boats, Beaches, Bars & Ballads)
TIJNMG	Tonight I Just Need My Guitar (Far Side of the World)

TLAH	Time Loves A Hero (Join the Band)
TLL	The Last Line (Son of a Son of a Sailor)
TLNP/K	The Legend of Norman Paperman/Kinja (Don't Stop the Carnival)
TM	The Missionary (Down to Earth/Jimmy Buffett/Before the Salt/Before the Beach/Collector's Edition: There's Nothing Soft About Hard Times/Best of the Early Years (Legend)/There's Nothing Soft About Hard Times/Captain America/Down to Earth-High Cumberland/Now Yer Squawkin')
TMOTTB	Take Me Out to the Ballgame (Live at Fenway Park/v/Live at Wrigley Field/v)
TMSAIS	That's My Story and I'm Stickin' to It (Off to See the Lizard/Live in Anguilla/v)
TNSAHT	There's Nothing Soft About Hard Times (Down to Earth/Jimmy Buffett/Before the Salt/Before the Beach/Collector's Edition: There's Nothing Soft About Hard Times/Best of the Early Years(Legend)/There's Nothing Soft About Hard Times/Captain America/ Singers, Songwriters, and Legends/Dow to Earth-High Cumberland/Now Yer Squawkin')
TNART	The Natives Are Restless Tonight (Live in Auburn/Live in Las Vegas/Live in Mansfield/Live in Cincinnati/Live in Hawaii)
TNIPTS	The Night I Painted the Sky (Barometer Soup)
TOTH	Trouble on the Horizon (Music for Our Mother Ocean, Volcano 2)
TPP	The Perfect Partner (Last Mango in Paris)
TRAV	Travelin' Clean (High Cumberland Jubilee/Before the Salt/Before the Beach/American Storyteller/Collector's Edition: There's Nothing Soft About Hard Times/Best of the Early Years (Legend)/There's Nothing Soft About Hard Times/Captain America/ Singers, Songwriters, and Legends/Down to Earth-High Cumberland/Now Yer Squawkin')
TS	Truckstop Salvation (Down to Earth/Jimmy Buffett/Before the Salt/Before the Beach/Col lector's Edition: There's Nothing Soft About Hard Times/Best of the Early Years (Legend)/There's Nothing Soft About Hard Times/Captain America/Singers, Songwriters, and Legends/Down to Earth-High Cumberland/Now Yer Squawkin')
TSB	The Same Boat (Wild in the Backyard)
TT	Tampico Trauma (Changes in Latitudes, Changes in Attitudes/You Had to Be There/Boats, Beaches, Bars & Ballads/Live in Auburn/Live in Cincinnati)
TTD	Train to Dixieland (Second Wind)
TTGH	Time to Go Home (Don't Stop the Carnival)
TTRWHS	Trying to Reason with Hurricane Season (A1A/Tuesdays, Thursdays, Saturdays/Encores)
TUR	Turnabout (Down to Earth/Jimmy Buffett/Before the Salt/American Storyteller/Collector's Edition: There's Nothing Soft About Hard Times/Best of the Early Years (Legend)/ There's Nothing Soft About Hard Times/Captain America)
TUTH	Turn Up the Heat and Chill the Rose (Buffet Hotel)
TVM	Twelve Volt Man (One Particular Harbour/Boats, Beaches, Bars & Ballads)
TW	The Wrangler (*Rancho Deluxe* Soundtrack)
TWAIK	The Wino and I Know (Living and Dying in ¾ Time/Live in: Vegas/Mansfield)
TWCM	The Wind Cries Mary (Live in Auburn)
TWIHIWYWB	The Weather is Here, I Wish You Were Beautiful (Coconut Telegraph/Boats, Beaches, Bars & Ballads)
TWLITM	That's What Living is to Me (Hot Water/Live in Anguilla/v)
UJB	Uncle John's Band (Fruitcakes)
UOTH	Up on the Hill (Don't Stop the Carnival)
UOTHT	Up on the House Top (Christmas Island)
USSZ	USS Zydecoldsmobile (Far Side of the World)
VOL	Volcano (Volcano/Songs You Know by Heart/Live by the Bay/Boats, Beaches, Bars Ballads The Parakeet Album/Biloxi/All the Great Hits/A Pirate's Treasure/ Tuesdays,Thursdays, Saturdays/Meet Me in Margaritaville/ Live in Auburn/Live in Las Vegas/Live in Mansfield/ Live in Cincinnati/Live in Hawaii/Live at Fenway Park/Live at Wrigley Field/Live in Anguilla/Scenes You Know by Heart/Nod to the Storyteller)
VMATHG	Vampires, Mummies and the Holy Ghost (Fruitcakes)
WATPOPWUA	We are the People Our Parents Warned Us About (One Particular Harbour/Live by the Bay/Meet Me in Margaritaville/Live in Hawaii)
WAWTTF	Who are We Trying to Fool (Don't Stop the Carnival)
WB	Wooly Bully (The Now Generation: Hits Are Our Business)
WBB	Wedding Bell Blues (The Now Generation: Hits Are Our Business)
WC	White Christmas ('Tis the SeaSon)

SONG CODES

WCT	Wonderful Christmastime ('Tis the SeaSon)
WDD	Whoop Dee Doo (Take the Weather With You)
WDWGDAS	Why Don't We Get Drunk (A White Sport Coat and A Pink Crustacean/ You Had to Be There/Songs You Know by Heart/Live by the Bay/Feeding Frenzy/ *The Doctor* Soundtrack/Boats, Beaches, Bars & Ballads/All the Great Hits /A Pirate's Treasure/ Where Were You When the Fun Stopped?/ Hed Kandi: The Acid Lounge Goes West/Meet Me in Margaritaville/Live in Auburn/Live in Las Vegas/Live in Mansfield/ Live in Cincinnati/ Live in Hawaii/Live at Fenway/Live at Wrigley Field/Scenes You Know by Heart/v)
WFTNE	Waiting for the Next Explosion (Beach House on the Moon)
WGCO	Woman Goin' Crazy on Caroline Street (Havana Daydreamin'/Live at Wrigley Field/v)
WIAW	Wheel Inside A Wheel (Take the Weather With You)
WIDG	What I Didn't Get for Christmas ('Tis the SeaSon)
WILD	Wildflowers (Encores)
WING	Wings (Buffet Hotel)
WITHP	What If the Hokey Pokey is All It Really is About (Far Side of the World)
WIV	Waiting in Vain (Live in Anguilla)
WLTBC	We Learned to be Cool from You (Buffet Hotel)
WNGB	West Nashville Grand Ballroom Gown (Living and Dying in ¾ Time)
WOL	Werewolves of London (*Hoot* Soundtrack)
WOTW	Window on the World (License to Chill)
WSPTD	When Salome Plays the Drum (Somewhere Over China/Boats, Beaches, Bars & Ballads/Live in Anguilla/v)
WTBS	Who's the Blonde Stranger (Riddles in the Sand/Live by the Bay/Boats, Beaches, Bars & Ballads/Tales from MargaritaVision)
WTCIC	When the Coast is Clear (Floridays/Boats, Beaches, Bars & Ballads)
WTP	Where's the Party (Somewhere Over China)
WTTW	Why the Things We Do (Off to See the Lizard)
WTWI	When This War is Over (Nod to the Storyteller)
WTWL	When the Wild Life Betrays Me (Riddles in the Sand)
WW	Winter Wonderland (Coral Reefer Christmas/'Tis the SeaSon)
WWTL	Wondering Where the Lions Are (*Hoot* Soundtrack)
WWWE	Wonder Why We N/Ever Go Home (Changes in Latitudes, Changes in Attitudes/You Had to Be There/*Rancho Deluxe* Soundtrack/Nod to the Storyteller)
WWY	Weather With You (Take the Weather With You/Live in Anguilla/v)
WYWH	Why You Wanna Hurt My Heart (One Particular Harbour/Nod to the Storyteller)
YCIJ	You Call It Jogging (Beach House on the Moon)
YLTLF	You've Lost That Lovin' Feeling (The Now Generation: Hits Are Our Business)
YNWIDB	You'll Never Work in Dis Bidness Again (Floridays/Feeding Frenzy)

DISCOGRAPHY

1969 – Heavy Dudes and Heartaches (45rpm: co-written Cason and Buffett) CAPRICE

1969 – Poopi Doo/Bluebird of Happiness (45rpm: Sun & the Tan Band) AUDIO MOBILE

1969 – Abandoned on Tuesday/Please Don't Bring Me Candy (45rpm) AUDIO MOBILE

1969 – The Now Generation: Hits Are Our Business SPAR RECORDS
SIDE ONE: 1. (Na Na, Hey Hey) Kiss Him Goodbye 2. A Brand New Me 3. Down on the Corner 4. Raindrops Keep Fallin' On My Head 5. Honky Tonk Woman 6. Wedding Bell Blues SIDE TWO: 7. You've Lost That Loving Feeling 8. It Must Be Him 9. Michelle 10. Wooly Bully 11. Groovin' 12. These Boots Are Made For Walkin'

1970 – The Now Generation: Come Together SPAR RECORDS
SIDE ONE: 1. Leaving On A Jet Plane 2. Sugar, Sugar 3. Someday We'll Be Together 4. Suspicious Minds 5. Come Together 6. Jean SIDE TWO: 1. Little Bit of Soul 2. Last Train to Clarksville 3. Never My Love 4. Oh, Pretty Woman 5. Sure Gonna Miss Her 6. My Bonnie

1970 – Down to Earth BARNABY
SIDE ONE: 1. The Christian? 2. Ellis Dee (He Ain't Free) 3. Richard Frost 4. The Missionary 5. A Mile High in Denver 6. The Captain and the Kid SIDE TWO: 7. Captain America 8. Ain't He A Genius 9.Turnaround 10. There's Nothin' Soft About Hard Times 11. I Can't Be Your Hero Today 12. Truckstop Salvation

1971 – Blessed Are . . . Joan Baez VANGUARD
Track 2. The Night They Drove Old Dixie Down (background vocals with Jerry Jeff Walker, Jimmy Buffett, *et al.*)

1972 – Somebody Else's Troubles Steve Goodman BUDDAH
Only in the literal sense of the word does Jimmy "appear" on Steve Goodman's second album. Seated alongside John Prine in the cover photo, Jimmy is identified only as "Marvin Gardens," but he is not credited for any performance on the recording. Though Jimmy had been mentioning "Marvin Gardens" as a member of his imaginary Coral Reefer Band in his live performances, this is the first time in print that the name actually appears in connection with Jimmy Buffett.

1973 – A White Sport Coat and a Pink Crustacean ABC-DUNHILL
SIDE ONE: 1. The Great Filling Station Holdup 2. Railroad Lady 3. He Went to Paris 4. Grapefruit-Juicy Fruit 5. Cuban Crime of Passion 6. Why Don't We Get Drunk SIDE TWO: 7. Peanut Butter Conspiracy 8. They Don't Dance Like Carmen No More 9. I Have Found Me A Home 10. My Lovely Lady 11. Death of an Unpopular Poet

1973 – Tarpon Soundtrack DVD **UYA** FILMS
An instrumental track of Brahma Fear does appear in this documentary.

1974 – Living and Dying in 3/4 Time ABC-DUNHILL
SIDE ONE: 1. Pencil Thin Mustache 2. Come Monday 3. Ringling Ringling 4. Brahma Fear 5. Brand New Country Star 6. Livingston's Gone to Texas SIDE TWO: 7. The Wino and I Know 8. West Nashville Grand Ballroom Gown 9. Saxophones 10. Ballad of Spider John 11. God's Own Drunk

1974 – A 1 A ABC-DUNHILL

SIDE ONE: 1. Makin' Music for Money 2. Door Number Three 3. Dallas 4. Presents to Send You 5. Stories We Could Tell 6. Life Is Just A Tire Swing SIDE TWO: 7. A Pirate Looks at Forty 8. Migration 9. Trying to Reason With Hurricane Season 10. Nautical Wheelers 11. Tin Cup Chalice

1975 – Rancho Deluxe Soundtrack LIBERTY/CAPITOL

SIDE ONE: 1. Rancho Deluxe 2. Ridin' in Style 3. Left Me With a Nail to Drive 4.Cattle Truckin' 5. Countin' the Cows Ev'ry Day 6. The Wrangler 7. Rancho Deluxe (End Title) SIDE TWO: 8. Livingston Saturday Night 9. Some Gothic Ranch Action 10. Wonder Why You Ever Go Home 11. Fifteen Gears 12. Can't Remember When I Slept Last 13. Rancho Deluxe (Instrumental)

1976 – Second Wind ABC

Apparently, this was the original title and release of the album which we know as **Havana Daydreamin'**, except that **Second Wind** included the songs "Please Take Your Drunken 15-Year-Old Girlfriend Home," as well as "Train to Dixieland." There are existing copies of **Havana Daydreamin'** which do include these two rare tracks without any listing; however, it's uncertain whether these are a recalled **Second Wind** album with a hasty **Havana Daydreamin'** label applied or **Havana Daydreamin'** recorded from a **Second Wind** unreleased master.

1976 – Havana Daydreamin' ABC

SIDE ONE: 1. Woman Goin' Crazy on Caroline Street 2. My Head Hurts, My Feet Stink, and I Don't Love Jesus 3. The Captain and the Kid 4. Big Rig 5. Defying Gravity SIDE TWO: 6. Havana Daydreamin' 7. Clichés 8. Something So Feminine About A Mandolin 9. Kick It In Second Wind 10. This Hotel Room

1977 – High Cumberland Jubilee (Recorded in 1972) BARNABY

SIDE ONE: 1. Ace 2. Rockefeller Square 3. Bend a Little 4. In the Shelter 5. Death Valley Lives 6.Cumberland High Dilemma 7. Livingston's Gone to Texas SIDE TWO: 8. England 9. Travelin' Clean 10. The Hangout Gang 11. God Don't Own a Car 12. High Cumberland Jubilee/Comin' Down Slow

1977 – Changes in Latitudes, Changes in Attitudes ABC

SIDE ONE: 1. Changes in Latitudes, Changes in Attitudes 2. Wonder Why We Ever Go Home 3.Banana Republics 4. Tampico Trauma 5. Lovely Cruise SIDE TWO: 6. Margaritaville 7. In the Shelter 8. Miss You So Badly 9. Biloxi 10. Landfall

1977 – Coast to Coast Soundtrack FULL MOON

Track 9. Survive - Jimmy Buffett

1977 – Solid Gold RONCO

Track 18. Margaritaville - Jimmy Buffett

1978 – Son of a Son of a Sailor ABC

SIDE ONE: 1. Son of a Son of a Sailor 2. Fool Button 3. The Last Line 4. Livingston Saturday Night 5. Cheeseburger in Paradise SIDE TWO: 6. Coast of Marseilles 7. Cowboy in the Jungle 8. Mañana 9. African Friend

1978 – You Had to Be There: Jimmy Buffett Live! MCA

DISC 1/SIDE ONE: 1. Son of a Son of a Sailor 2. Pencil Thin Mustache 3. Wonder Why We Ever Go Home 4. Landfall 5. Miss You So Badly SIDE TWO: 6. Havana Daydreamin' 7. Margaritaville 8. Changes in Latitudes 9. Come Monday 10. Perrier Blues
DISC 2/SIDE ONE: 1. Grapefruit-Juicy Fruit 2. God's Own Drunk 3. He Went to Paris 4. The Captain and the Kid SIDE TWO: 5. Why Don't We Get Drunk (And Screw) 6. A Pirate Looks at Forty 7. Tampico Trauma 8. Morris' Nightmare 9. Dixie Diner

1978 – FM Soundtrack MCA

DISC 2/SIDE ONE: 3. Livingston Saturday Night - Jimmy Buffett

1979 – Volcano MCA

SIDE ONE: 1. Fins 2. Volcano 3. Treat Her Like A Lady 4. Stranded on a Sandbar 5. Chanson Pour Les Petits Enfants SIDE TWO: 6. Survive 7. Lady I Can't Explain 8. Boat Drinks 9. Dreamsicle 10. Sending the Old Man Home

1982 – The Long Run - Eagles ASYLUM

SIDE TWO: 9. The Greeks Don't Want No Freaks - Don Henley, lead vocals (background vocals by "The Monstertones," including "Freddy" Buffett)

1979 – Before the Salt BARNABY

[Down to Earth] DISC 1/SIDE ONE: 1. The Christian? 2. Ellis Dee 3. Richard Frost 4. The Missionary 5. A Mile High in Denver 6. The Captain and the Kid SIDE TWO: 7. Captain America 8. Ain't He A Genius 9. Turnabout 10. There's Nothin' Soft About Hard Times 11. I Can't Be Your Hero 12. Truckstop Salvation

[High Cumberland Jubilee] DISC 2/SIDE ONE: 1. Ace 2. Rockefeller Square 3. Bend a Little 4. In the Shelter 5. Death Valley Lives 6. Cumberland High Dilemma SIDE TWO: 7. Livingston's Gone to Texas 8. England 9. Travelin' Clean 10. The Hangout Gang 11. God Don't Own a Car 12. High Cumberland Jubilee/Comin' Down Slow

1980 – *Urban Cowboy* Soundtrack ELEKTRA/ASYLUM

SIDE ONE: Track 1. Hello Texas - Jimmy Buffett

1981 – Coconut Telegraph MCA

SIDE ONE: 1. Coconut Telegraph 2. Incommunicado 3. It's My Job 4. Growing Older, But Not Up 5. The Good Fight SIDE TWO: 6. The Weather Is Here, Wish You Were Beautiful 7. Stars Fell on Alabama 8. Island 9. Little Miss Magic

1981 – Dad Loves His Work - James Taylor COLUMBIA

Track 9. Sugar Trade - James Taylor (co-written with Jimmy Buffett and Timothy Mayer)

1981 – Jane Fonda's Workout Tape SONY MUSIC

Track 6. Changes in Latitudes, Changes in Attitudes - Jimmy Buffett

1982 – Somewhere Over China MCA

SIDE ONE: 1. Where's the Party 2. It's Midnight and I'm Not Famous Yet 3. I Heard I Was in Town 4. Somewhere over China SIDE TWO: 5. When Salome Plays the Drum 6. Lip Service 7. If I Could Just Get It on Paper 8. Steamer 9. On A Slow Boat to China

1982 – Jimmy Buffett EXCELSIOR

[Down to Earth] SIDE ONE: 1. The Christian? 2. Turnabout 3. Richard Frost 4. The Missionary 5. A Mile High in Denver 6. The Captain and the Kid SIDE TWO: 7. Captain America 8. Ain't He A Genius 9. Ellis Dee (He Ain't Free) 10. There's Nothin' Soft About Hard Times 11. I Can't Be Your Hero 12. Truckstop Salvation

1982 – *Fast Times at Ridgemont High* Soundtrack ELEKTRA/ASYLUM

DISC 2/SIDE ONE: Track 1. I Don't Know (Spicoli's Theme) - Jimmy Buffett

1982 – No Fun Aloud - Glen Frey ASYLUM

Track 3. Partytown - Glen Frey, lead vocals (background vocals by "The Monstertones," including "Freddy" Buffett)

1983 – One Particular Harbour MCA

SIDE ONE: 1. Stars on the Water 2. I Used to Have Money One Time 3. Livin' It Up 4. California Promises 5. One Particular Harbor SIDE TWO: 6. Why You Wanna Hurt My Heart? 7. Honey Do 8. We Are the People (Our Parents Warned Us About) 9. Twelve Volt Man 10. Brown-Eyed Girl 11. Distantly in Love

1984 – Riddles in the Sand MCA

SIDE ONE: 1. Who's the Blonde Stranger? 2. When the Wild Life Betrays Me 3. Ragtop Day 4. She's Going Out of My Mind 5. Bigger That the Both of Us SIDE TWO: 6. Knees of My Heart 7. Come to the Moon 8. Love in Decline 9. Burn That Bridge 10. La Vie Dansante

1985 – Songs You Know by Heart: Jimmy Buffett's Greatest Hit(s) MCA
SIDE ONE: 1. Cheeseburger in Paradise 2. He Went to Paris 3. Fins 4. Son of a Son of a Sailor 5. A Pirate Looks at Forty 6. Margaritaville SIDE TWO: 7. Come Monday 8. Changes in Latitudes, Changes in Attitudes 9. Why Don't We Get Drunk 10. Pencil Thin Mustache 11. Grapefruit-Juicy Fruit 12. Boat Drinks 13. Volcano

1985 – Last Mango in Paris MCA
SIDE ONE: 1. Everybody's on the Run 2. Frank & Lola 3. Perfect Partner 4. Please Bypass This Heart 5. Gypsies in the Palace SIDE TWO: 6. Desperation Samba 7. If the Phone Doesn't Ring, It's Me 8. Last Mango in Paris 9. Jolly Mon Sing 10. Beyond the End

1985 – *The Slugger's Wife* Soundtrack MCA
SIDE ONE: Track 8. Ragtop Day - Jimmy Buffett

1985 – *Summer Rental* Soundtrack PARAMOUNT
End Theme: Turning Around - Jimmy Buffett

1985 – Tennessee Christmas UNIVERSAL SPECIAL PRODUCTS
SIDE TWO: Track 8. Christmas in the Caribbean - Jimmy Buffett

1986 – Floridays MCA
SIDE ONE: 1. I Love the Now 2. Creola 3. First Look 4. Meet Me in Memphis 5. Nobody Speaks to the Captain SIDE TWO: 6. Floridays 7. If It All Falls Down 8. No Plane on Sunday 9. When the Coast Is Clear 10. You'll Never Work In Dis Bidness Again

1986 – Live by the Bay (Video) MCA
1. Door Number Three 2. Grapefruit-Juicy Fruit 3. We Are the People (Our Parents Warned Us About) 4. Stars on the Water 5. Coconut Telegraph 6. Come Monday 7. Ragtop Day 8. Who's the Blonde Stranger? 9. Volcano 10. Changes in Latitudes, Changes in Attitudes 11. One Particular Harbour 12. If the Phone Doesn't Ring, It's Me 13. Why Don't We Get Drunk 14. Cheeseburger in Paradise 15. Fins 16. Last Mango in Paris 17. A Pirate Looks at Forty 18. Margaritaville

1988 – Hot Water MCA
SIDE ONE: 1. Homemade Music 2. Baby's Gone Shoppin' 3. Bring Back the Magic 4. My Barracuda 5. L'Air de la Louisiane SIDE TWO: 6. Prince of Tides 7. Pre-You 8. King of Somewhere Hot 9. Great Heart 10. Smart Woman (In a Real Short Skirt) 11. That's What Living Is to Me

1988 – Tennessee Christmas UNIVERSAL
SIDE TWO: Track 8. Christmas in the Caribbean - Jimmy Buffett

1989 – Off to See the Lizard MCA
SIDE ONE: 1. Carnival World 2. Take Another Road 3. That's My Story and I'm Stickin' to It 4. Why the Things We Do 5. Gravity Storm 6. Off to See the Lizard SIDE TWO: 7. Boomerang Love 8. Strange Bird 9. I Wish Lunch Could Last Forever 10. The Pascagoula Run 11. Mermaid in the Night 12. Changing Channels

1989 – Neville Brothers & Friends: Tell It Like It Is (Video) IMAGE ENTERTAINMENT
Track 11. Middle of the Night - Jimmy Buffett and the Neville Brothers

1990 – *Always* Soundtrack MCA
SIDE ONE: Track 2. Boomerang Love - Jimmy Buffett

1990 – *Arachnophobia* Soundtrack ATLANTIC/ELEKTRA/ASYLUM
SIDE TWO: Track 13. Don't Bug Me - Jimmy Buffett

1990 – Women in the Room - Zachary Richard A&M
Track 1. Who Stole My Monkey - Zachary Richard with Jimmy Buffett on background vocals

1990 – Feeding Frenzy MCA
1. You'll Never Work In Dis Bidness Again 2. The City 3. Last Mango in Paris 4. Come Monday 5. Today's Message 6. A Love Song (From a Different Point of View) 7. One Particular Harbour 8. Honey Do 9. Cheeseburger in Paradise 10. A Pirate Looks at Forty 11. Jolly Mon Sing 12. Gypsies in the Palace 13. Fins 14. Margaritaville 15. Jamaica Farewell 16. Volcano

1992 – *Ferngully: The Last Rainforest* **Soundtrack** MCA
Track 3. If I'm Gonna Eat Somebody (It Might As Well Be You) - Ton Loc (written by Buffett/Utley)

1992 – Boats, Beaches, Bars & Ballads (Boxed Set) MCA
DISC 1 - BOATS: 1. Son of a Son of a Sailor 2. Havana Daydreamin' 3. Mañana 4. Treat Her Like A Lady 5. Steamer 6. Jolly Mon Sing 7. Nautical Wheelers 8. Take It Back 9. On A Slow Boat to China 10. Changes in Latitudes, Changes in Attitudes 11. Love and Luck 12. The Captain & the Kid 13. Trying to Reason With Hurricane Season 14. Boat Drinks 15. One Particular Harbour 16. A Pirate Looks at Forty 17. Lovely Cruise
DISC 2 - BEACHES: 1. Margaritaville 2. Grapefruit-Juicy Fruit 3. Ragtop Day 4. Frank and Lola 5. Tin Cup Chalice 6. Knees of My Heart 7. Money Back Guarantee 8. When the Coast Is Clear 9. Biloxi 10. Distantly in Love 11. Coconut Telegraph 12. Stars on the Water 13. Who's the Blonde Stranger? 14. I Have Found Me A Home 15. Christmas in the Caribbean 16. Volcano 17. Brown Eyed Girl 18. Cheeseburger in Paradise
DISC 3 - BARS: 1. Fins 2. The Weather Is Here, I Wish You Were Beautiful 3. Tampico Trauma 4. Livingston Saturday Night 5. Cuban Crime of Passion 6. First Look 7. The Wino and I Know 8. Great Filling Station Holdup 9. Why Don't We Get Drunk (And Screw) 10. Elvis Imitators 11. Pencil Thin Mustache 12. Kick It In, Second Wind 13. Desperation Samba 14. When Salome Plays the Drum 15. They Don't Dance Like Carmen No More 16. The Pascagoula Run 17. Sending the Old Man Home 18. Domino College
DISC 4 - BALLADS: 1. Come Monday 2. Defying Gravity 3. Survive 4. Incommunicado 5. I Heard I Was in Town 6. Ballad of Spider John 7. Little Miss Magic 8. California Promises 9. If the Phone Doesn't Ring, It's Me 10. African Friend 11. Everlasting Moon 12. Pre-You 13. Middle of the Night 14. Coast of Marseilles 15. Island 16. He Went to Paris 17. Stars Fell on Alabama 18. Changing Channels 19. Twelve Volt Man

1993 – More Songs for Sleepless Nights SONY
Track 11. Stars Fell on Alabama - Jimmy Buffett

1993 – *Johnny Bago* **Theme** CBS TELEVISION

1993 – *The Firm* **Soundtrack** GRP
Track 2. Stars on the Water - Jimmy Buffett

1993 – No Time to Kill - Clint Black RCA
Track 9. Happiness Alone - Clint Black (co-written with Jimmy Buffett)

1993 – Before the Beach MARGARITAVILLE
1. Ellis Dee (He Ain't Free) 2. The Missionary 3. A Mile High in Denver 4. The Captain & the Kid 5. Captain America 6. Turnabout 7. There's Nothin' Soft About Hard Times 8. I Can't Be Your Hero Today 9. Truckstop Salvation 10. Ace 11. Rockefeller Square 12. Bend a Little 13. In the Shelter 14. Death Valley Lives 15. Livingston's Gone to Texas 16. England 17. Travelin' Clean 18. The Hangout Gang 19. God Don't Own a Car 20. High Cumberland Jubilee/Comin' Down Slow 21. Cumberland High Dilemma

1993 – Margaritaville Café Late Night Menu MCA
Track 7. Another Saturday Night - Jimmy Buffett 11. Some White People Can Dance - Greg "Fingers" Taylor (co-written by Taylor, Buffett, Krekel, Utley) 17. Reggae Accident - Jimmy Buffett 20. Souvenirs - Jimmy Buffett

1994 – Duets II CAPITOL
Track 11. Mack the Knife - Frank Sinatra and Jimmy Buffett

1994 – Fruitcakes MCA
1. Everybody's Got a Cousin in Miami 2. Fruitcakes 3. Lone Palm 4. Six String Music 5. Uncle John's Band 6. Love in the Library 7. Quietly Making Noise 8. Frenchman for the Night 9. Sunny Afternoon 10. Vampires, Mummies and the Holy Ghost 11. She's Got You 12. Delaney Talks to Statues 13. Apocalypso

DISCOGRAPHY

1994 – The Same Boat
Track recorded for **Fruitcakes**. Co-written with Don Henry and Carol Ann Etheridge.

1995 – Margaritaville Café - New Orleans / Late Night Gumbo MARGARITAVILLE
Track 5. Sea Cruise - Jimmy Buffett 15. Goodnight Irene - Jimmy Buffett

1995 – Barometer Soup MARGARITAVILLE/MCA
1. Barometer Soup 2. Barefoot Children in the Rain 3. Bank of Bad Habits 4. Remittance Man 5. Diamond as Big as the Ritz 6. Blue Heaven Rendezvous 7. Jimmy Dreams 8. Lage Nom Ai 9. Don't Chu Know 10. Ballad of Skip Wiley 11. The Night I Painted the Sky 12. Mexico

1995 – Duets, Vols. 1 & 2 DCC
Disc 2/Track 11. Mack the Knife- Frank Sinatra and Jimmy Buffett

1995 – Kermit Unpigged BMG
Track 6. Mr. Spaceman - Jimmy Buffett and The Great Gonzo

1995 - The Parakeet Album: Songs of Jimmy Buffett MARGARITAVILLE
1. Christmas in the Caribbean 2. Volcano 3. La Vie Dansante 4. Jolly Mon Sing 5. Little Miss Magic 6. Cheeseburger in Paradise 7. Off to See the Lizard 8. Chanson Pour Les Petits Enfants 9. Come to the Moon 10. Delaney Talks to Statues

1996 – Banana Wind MARGARITAVILLE/MCA
1. Only Time Will Tell 2. Jamaica Mistaica 3. School Boy Heart 4. Banana Wind 5. Holiday 6. Bob Robert's Society Band 7. Overkill 8. Desdemona's Building a Rocket Ship 9. Mental Floss 10. Cultural Infidel 11. Happily Ever After (Now and Then) 12. False Echoes (Havana 1921) 13. [Unlisted] Treetop Flyer

1996 – Christmas Island MARGARITAVILLE/MCA
1. Christmas Island 2. Jingle Bells 3. A Sailor's Christmas 4. Happy Xmas (War Is Over) 5. Up on the House Top 6. Mele Kalikimaka 7. Run Rudolph Run 8. Ho Ho Ho and a Bottle of Rhum 9. I'll Be Home for Christmas 10. Merry Christmas, Alabama (Never Far from Home)

1996 – Great American Summer Fun with Jimmy Buffett MCA SPECIAL PRODUCTS
1. Come Monday 2. Changes in Latitudes, Changes in Attitudes 3. Cheeseburger in Paradise 4. One Particular Harbour 5. Bank of Bad Habits 6. Fruitcakes 7. Brown-Eyed Girl

1997 – *Contact* WARNER BROTHERS DVD [NOT ON THE SOUNDTRACK CD]
Purple People Eater - Jimmy Buffett

1997 – M.O.M., Vol. 2: Music for Our Mother Ocean INTERSCOPE
Track 17. Trouble on the Horizon - Jimmy Buffett

1997 – Uptown - Neville Brothers EMI
Track 9. Midnight Key - Neville Brothers (written by Jimmy Buffett)

1997 – Music for Montserrat (Video) IMAGES ENTERTAINMENT
Track 8. Volcano - Jimmy Buffett 17. Hey Jude - Paul McCartney with Jimmy Buffett, Eric Clapton, Phil Collins, Elton John, Mark Knopfler, Carl Perkins, Sting

1998 – Don't Stop the Carnival POLYGRAM
1. Introduction: The Legend of Norman Paperman/Kinja 2. Public Relations 3. Calaloo 4. Island Fever 5. Sheila Says 6. Just an Old Truth Teller 7. Henny's Song: The Key to My Man 8. Kinja Rules 9. A Thousand Steps to Nowhere 10. It's All About the Water 11. Champagne Si, Agua No 12. Public Relations (Reprise) 13. The Handiest Frenchman in the Caribbean 14. Hippolyte's Habitat 15. Who Are We Trying to Fool? 16. Fat Person Man 17. Up on the Hill 18. Domicile 19. Funeral Dance 20. Time to Go Home 21. [ENHANCED TRACK: Green Flash at Midnight]

1998 – Biloxi PREMIUM MUSIC
1. Margaritaville 2. Cheeseburger in Paradise 3. Son of a Son of a Sailor 4. Livingston Saturday Night 5. Biloxi 6. Mañana 7. Changes in Latitudes 8. The Great Filling Station Holdup 9. Brand New Country Star 10. Coconut Telegraph 11. Fins 12. A Pirate Looks at Forty 13. Havana Day-

dreamin' 14. Volcano 15. Last Mango in Paris 16. Grapefruit-Juicy Fruit 17. California Promises

1998 – Evangeline MCA
Track 7. Gulf Coast Highway - Evangeline and Jimmy Buffett

1998 – Jimmy Buffett: All the Great Hits PRISM LEISURE
1. Margaritaville 2. Fins 3. Come Monday 4. Volcano 5. Changes in Latitudes,Changes in Attitudes 6. Cheeseburger in Paradise 7. Son of a Son of a Sailor 8. Stars Fell on Alabama 9. Miss You So Badly 10. Why Don't We Get Drunk 11. A Pirate Looks at Forty 12. He Went to Paris 13. Grapefruit-Juicy Fruit 14. Pencil Thin Mustache 15. Boat Drinks 16. Chanson Pour Les Petits Enfants 17. Banana Republics 18. Last Mango in Paris

1998 – A Pirate's Treasure: 20 Jimmy Buffett Gems MCA
1. Son of a Son of a Sailor 2. Margaritaville 3. Grapefruit-Juicy Fruit 4. A Pirate Looks at Forty 5. Come Monday 6. Pencil Thin Mustache 7. Changes in Latitudes 8. Nautical Wheelers 9. Coast of Marseilles 10. Jolly Mon Sing 11. He Went to Paris 12. Mañana 13. Little Miss Magic 14. African Friend 15. Volcano 16. On a Slow Boat to China 17. Stars Fell on Alabama 18. Livingston Saturday Night 19. One Particular Harbour 20. Why Don't We Get Drunk

1998 – Elmopalooza! SONY/SONY WONDER/CHILDREN'S TELEVISION
Track 8. Caribbean Amphibian - Jimmy Buffett and the All-Amphibian Band

1998 – Imagination - Brian Wilson WARNER BROTHERS
Track 3. South America - Brian Wilson and Jimmy Buffett

1999 – Beach House on the Moon POLYGRAM
1. Beach House on the Moon 2. Permanent Reminder of a Temporary Feeling 3. Waiting for the Next Explosion 4. Pacing the Cage 5. You Call It Jogging 6. Flesh and Bone 7. I Will Play for Gumbo 8. Math Suks 9. Spending Money 10. Semi-True Story 11. Lucky Stars 12. I Don't Know and I Don't Care 13. Oysters and Pearls 14. [CD-ROM TRACK]

1999 – Word of Mouth - Mac McAnally DREAMWORKS
Track 4. The Ass and the Hole - Mac McAnally and Jimmy Buffett

1999 Buffett Live: Tuesdays, Thursdays, Saturdays MAILBOAT
1. Fruitcakes 2. Southern Cross 3. Pencil Thin Mustache 4. Trying to Reason with Hurricane Season 5. Coconut Telegraph 6. Cheeseburger in Paradise 7. Come Monday 8. Son of a Son of a Sailor 9. Volcano 10. Brown-Eyed Girl 11. Tin Cup Chalice 12. Fins 13. One Particular Harbour 14. Margaritaville 15. Love and Luck [ENHANCED TRACK] Backstage with Buffett

1999 – Under the Influence - Alan Jackson ARISTA
Track 12. Margaritaville - Alan Jackson and Jimmy Buffett

1999 – Beach Music Anthology, Vol. 2 RIPETE
DISC 2/TRACK 1. In the Shelter - Jimmy Buffett

1999 – M.O.M., Vol. 3: Music for Our Mother Ocean HOLLYWOOD
Track 12. Sea Cruise - Jimmy Buffett

1999 – Where Were You When the Fun Stopped? EMI
Track 13. Why Don't We Get Drunk - Jimmy Buffett

1999 – American Storyteller DELTA
1. The Christian? 2. Ellis Dee (He Ain't Free) 3. Richard Frost 4. A Mile High in Denver 5. The Captain and the Kid 6. Captain America 7. Ain't He A Genius 8. Turnabout 9. I Can't Be Your Hero Today 10. Livingston's Gone to Texas 11. Traveling Clean 12. God Don't Own a Car

1999 – Collector's Edition: There's Nothing Soft About Hard Times MADACY
DISC 1: 1. There's Nothin' Soft About Hard Times 2. Traveling Clean 3. Livingston's Gone to Texas 4. I Can't Be Your Hero Today 5. God Don't Own a Car 6. The Captain and the Kid

7. A Mile High in Denver 8. Ain't He A Genius 9. Captain America 10. High Cumberland Jubilee/Coming Down Slow 11. Rockefeller Square 12. Truckstop Salvation
DISC 2: 1. Ace 2. Bend a Little 3. The Christian? 4. Cumberland High Dilemma
5. Death Valley Lives 6. Ellis Dee 7. The Hangout Gang 8. In the Shelter 9. The Missionary 10. Richard Frost 11. Turnabout

1999 – Calaloo Best Buy Exclusive MARGARITAVILLE
1. Kinja 2. Cheeseburger In Paradise 3 Stories from My Favorite Books [That's What
Living is to Me] 4. Island Fever 5. Cairo 6. Come Monday

2000 – Best of the Early Years DELTA
1. The Missionary 2. Truckstop Salvation 3. Ace 4. Rockefeller Square 5. Bend a Little
6. In the Shelter 7. Death Valley Lives 8. Cumberland High Dilemma 9. The Hangout
Gang 10. High Cumberland Jubilee 11. There's Nothin' Soft About Hard Times

2000 – There's Nothing Soft About Hard Times MADACY
1. There's Nothin' Soft About Hard Times 2. Traveling Clean 3. Livingston's Gone to
Texas 4. I Can't Be Your Hero Today 5. God Don't Own a Car 6. The Captain and the
Kid 7. Mile High in Denver 8. Ain't He A Genius 9. Captain America 10. High Cumberland Jubilee/ Coming Down Slow 11. Rockefeller Square 12. Truckstop Salvation

2000 – Best of the Early Years LEGEND
DISC 1: 1. The Missionary 2. Truckstop Salvation 3. Ace 4. Rockefeller Square 5. Bend a Little
6. In the Shelter 7. Death Valley Lives 8. Cumberland High Dilemma 9. The Hangout Gang
10. High Cumberland Jubilee? 11. There's Nothin' Soft About Hard Times
DISC 2: 1. The Christian? 2. Ellis Dee (He Ain't Free) 3. Richard Frost 4. A Mile High in Denver
5. The Captain and the Kid 6. Captain America 7. Ain't He A Genius 8. Turnabout 9. I Can't Be
Your Hero Today 10. Livingston's Gone to Texas 11. Traveling Clean 12. God Don't Own a Car

2000 – Tales from MargaritaVision (Video) MAILBOAT/MCA VIDEO
1. Pencil Thin Mustache 2. Come Monday 3. He Went to Paris 4. Nautical Wheelers 5. Livin' It
Up 6. One Particular Harbour 7. La Vie Dansante 8. Who's the Blonde Stranger? 9. Homemade
Music 10. Take Another Road 11. Jamaica Farewell 12. Another Saturday Night 13. Fruitcakes
14. Changes in Latitudes, Changes in Attitudes (live) 15. The City (live)

2000 – Club Trini Margaritaville Café Late Night Menu in New Orleans MAILBOAT
Track 6. African Friend - Jimmy Buffett 7. Come On In - Jimmy Buffett 8. Cairo - Jimmy Buffett & Nadirah Shakoor 12. No Woman, No Cry - Jimmy Buffett

2001 – Sharin' in the Groove: Celebrating the Music of Phish MOCKINGBIRD
DISC 1: Track 2. Gumbo - Jimmy Buffett

2001 – Today [Show] Presents: The Best of the Today Concert Series, Vol. 2 NBC
Track 9. Fins - Jimmy Buffett

2002 – Captain America MADACY
DISC 1: 1. There's Nothing Soft About Hard Times 2. Traveling Clean 3. Livingston's Gone to
Texas 4. I Can't Be Your Hero Today 5. God Don't Own a Car 6. The Captain and the Kid 7. A
Mile High in Denver 8. Ain't He A Genius 9. Captain America 10. High Cumberland Jubilee/
Coming Down Slow 11. Rockefeller Square 12. Truckstop Salvation
DISC 2: 1. Ace 2. Bend a Little 3. The Christian? 4. Cumberland High Dilemma 5. Death Valley
Lives 6. Ellis Dee 7. The Hangout Gang 8. In the Shelter 9. The Missionary 10. Richard Frost
11. Turnabout

2002 – Far Side of the World MAILBOAT
1. Blue guitar 2. Mademoiselle (Voulez-Vous Danser) 3. Autour du Rocher 4. Savannah Fare
You Well 5. All the Ways I Want You 6. Last Man Standing 7. What if the Hokey-Pokey Is All It
Really Is About? 8. Altered Boy 9. USS Zydecoldsmobile 10. Someday I Will 11. Far Side of the
World 12. Tonight I Just Need My Guitar

2002 – Singers, Songwriters, and Legends MADACY SPECIAL PRODUCTS
DISC 1: 1. There's Nothing Soft About Hard Times 2. Traveling Clean 3. Livingston's Gone to Texas 4. I Can't Be Your Hero Today 5. God Don't Own A Car 6. The Captain and the Kid 7. A Mile High in Denver 8. Ain't He A Genius 9. Captain America 10. High Cumberland Jubilee/Coming Down Slow 11. Rockefeller Square 12. Truckstop Salvation

2002 – Forever Tams BRADLEY HOUSE RECORDS
Track 10. Flesh and Bone - Jimmy Buffett and The Tams

2002 – One of These Nights TRADE LINE
Track 8. Volcano - Don Henley and Jimmy Buffett 10. Margaritaville - Don Henley and Jimmy Buffett

2002 – Tennessee Christmas DELTA
Track 8. Christmas in the Caribbean - Jimmy Buffett

2003 – All the Great Hits PRISM LEISURE
1. Margaritaville 2. Fins 3. Come Monday 4. Volcano 5. Changes in Latitudes, Changes in Attitude 6. Cheeseburger in Paradise 7. Son of a Son of a Sailor 8. Stars Fell on Alabama 9. Miss You So Badly 10. Why Don't We Get Drunk 11. A Pirate Looks at Forty 12. He Went to Paris 13. Grapefruit-Juicy Fruit 14. Pencil Thin Mustache 15. Boat Drinks 16. Chanson Pours Les Petits Enfants 17. Banana Republic 18. Last Mango in Paris

2003 – Meet Me in Margaritaville: The Ultimate Collection MCA
DISC 1: 1. Margaritaville 2. Migration 3. Growing Older, But Not Up 4. Holiday 5. Come Monday 6. Fruitcakes 7. We Are the People (Our Parents Warned Us About) 8. Cheeseburger in Paradise 9. Jolly Mon Sing 10. The Pascagoula Run 11. Tin Cup Chalice 12. Pencil Thin Moustache [sic] 13. Grapefruit/Juicy Fruit 14. Coconut Telegraph 15. Changes in Latitudes, Changes in Attitudes 16. Last Mango in Paris 17. Fins 18. Why Don't We Get Drunk 19. Brown-Eyed Girl 20. One Particular Harbour
DISC 2: 1. School Boy Heart 2. Everybody's Talkin' 3. Volcano 4. Son of a Son of a Sailor (new recording) 5. Take Another Road 6. Knees of My Heart 7. In the Shelter 8. Havana Daydreamin' 9. Desperation Samba [Live] 10. Barefoot Children 11. Saxophones (new recording) 12. Cowboy in the Jungle 13. He Went to Paris 14. Creola 15. Bob Robert's Society Band 16. A Pirate Looks at Forty [Live] 17. Sail on Sailor 18. The Captain and the Kid

2003 – Alan Jackson: Greatest Hits, Vol. 2 - Alan Jackson ARISTA
DISC 1: Track 17. It's Five O'Clock Somewhere - Alan Jackson and Jimmy Buffett

2003 – Live in Auburn, WA MAILBOAT
DISC 1: 1. Great Heart 2. Saxophones 3. Gypsies in the Palace 4. In the Shelter 5. Grapefruit-Juicy Fruit 6. Son of a Son of a Sailor 7. Knees of My Heart 8. Burn That Bridge 9. Come Monday 10. The Natives Are Restless Tonight 11. It's Five O'Clock Somewhere 12. One Particular Harbour 13. Cheeseburger in Paradise
DISC 2: 1 The Tiki Bar is Open 2. Everybody's Talkin' 3. Why Don't We Get Drunk (And Screw) 4. I Still Miss Someone 5. It's My Job 6. I Don't Know (Spicoli's Theme) 7. A Pirate Looks at Forty 8. Changes in Latitudes, Changes in Attitudes 9. Tampico Trauma 10. Mexico 11. Margaritaville 12. Volcano 13. Fins 14. Far Side of the World 15. The Wind Cries Mary

2003 – Live in Las Vegas, NV MAILBOAT
DISC 1: 1. Great Heart 2. It's Midnight and I'm Not Famous Yet 3. Gypsies in the Palace 4. In the Shelter 5. Jolly Mon Sing 6. Son of a Son of a Sailor 7. Come Monday 8. Gravity Storm 9. Pencil Thin Mustache 10. The Natives Are Restless Tonight 11. It's Five O'Clock Somewhere 12. One Particular Harbour 13. Cheeseburger in Paradise
DISC 2: 1. The Tiki Bar is Open 2. Everybody's Talkin' 3. Why Don't We Get Drunk 4. This Hotel Room 5. The Wino and I Know 6. School Boy Heart 7. I Don't Know (Spicoli's Theme) 8. A Pirate Looks at Forty 9. Changes in Latitudes, Changes in Attitudes 10. Mexico 11. Margaritaville 12. Volcano 13. Fins 14. Southern Cross 15. Brown Eyed Girl 16. Lovely Cruise

DISCOGRAPHY

2003 – Hed Kandi: The Acid Lounge Goes West ACID LOUNGE
DISC 2: Track 14. Why Don't We Get Drunk - Jimmy Buffett

2003 – Love Flashback Collection CUTTING
DISC 13: Track 11. Survive - Jimmy Buffett

2003 – *Hollywood's Magic Island: Catalina* **Soundtrack** BLUE WATER ENTERTAINMENT
Track 17. Son of A Son of A Sailor - Jimmy Buffett

2003 – *Anger Management* **Soundtrack** DVD SONY PICTURES HOME ENTERTAINMENT
Track 2. Margaritaville - Jimmy Buffett

2003 – Now That's What I Call Christmas! The Signature Collection CAPITOL
DISC 1: Track 7. Jingle Bells - Jimmy Buffett

2003 – MiniMatinee #1 (Video) MAILBOAT
1. It's Five O'Clock Somewhere - Alan Jackson and Jimmy Buffett 2. Cheeseburger in Paradise 3. Meet Me in Margaritaville 4. The Tiki Bar is Open 5. Knees of My Heart - Acoustic rehearsal performance by Jimmy Buffett, Peter Mayer, and Ralph McDonald 6. Fins 7. Dress rehearsal version of The Tiki Bar Is Open

2004 – Legends: We Will Rock You TIME-LIFE
Track 20. Margaritaville - Jimmy Buffett

2004 – Everglades Trail WILDERNESS GRAPHICS INC.
Track 1. Bob Robert's Society Band - Jimmy Buffett 12. Ballad Of Skip Wiley - Jimmy Buffett

2004 – *Sports Illustrated* **Swimsuit Edition DVD** MAILBOAT
License to Chill - Jimmy Buffett and Kenny Chesney

2004 – *Rancho Deluxe* **Soundtrack [2004]** VARESE
1. Rancho Deluxe 2. Ridin' in Style 3. Left Me With a Nail to Drive 4. Cattle Truckin' 5. Countin' the Cows Ev'ry Day 6. The Wrangler 7. Rancho Deluxe (End Title) 8. Livingston Saturday Night 9. Some Gothic Ranch Action 10. Wonder Why You Ever Go Home 11. Fifteen Gears 12. Can't Remember When I Slept Last 13. Rancho Deluxe

2004 – The Great Jimmy Buffett GOLDIES
1. The Great Filling Station Holdup 2. Railroad Lady 3. He Went to Paris 4. Grapefruit-Juicy Fruit 5. Cuban Crime of Passion 6. Why Don't We Get Drunk 7. Peanut Butter Conspiracy 8. They Don't Dance Like Carmen No More 9. I Have Found Me A Home 10. My Lovely Lady 11. Death of An Unpopular Poet 12. Ringling, Ringling 13. Brand New Country Star 14. God's Own Drunk

2004 – Live in Mansfield, MA MAILBOAT
DISC 1: 1. Great Heart 2. Gravity Storm 3. Gypsies in the Palace 4. In the Shelter 5. Honey Do 6.Son of a Son of a Sailor 7. Knees of My Heart 8. Coconut Telegraph 9. The Natives Are Restless 10. Come Monday 11. It's Five O'Clock Somewhere 12. One Particular Harbour 13. Cheeseburger in Paradise
DISC 2: 1. Tiki Bar is Open 2. Everybody's Talkin' 3. Why Don't We Get Drunk 4. The Wino and I Know 5. It's My Job 6. School Boy Heart 7. Pirate Looks at Forty 8. Changes in Latitudes, Changes in Attitudes 9. Apocalypso 10. Mexico 11. Margaritaville 12. Volcano 13. Fins 14. Sea Cruise 15. Lovely Cruise

2004 – Live in Cincinnati, OH MAILBOAT
DISC 1: 1. Great Heart 2. Gypsies in the Palace 3. Saxophones 4. In the Shelter 5. Honey Do 6. Son of a Son of a Sailor 7. Knees of My Heart 8. Burn That Bridge 9. Natives Are Restless 10. Come Monday 11. It's 5 O'Clock Somewhere 12. One Particular Harbour 13. Cheeseburger in Paradise
DISC 2: 1. Tiki Bar is Open 2. Everybody's Talkin' 3. Why Don't We Get Drunk 4. This Hotel Room 5. It's My Job 6. Tampico Trauma 7. Pirate Looks at Forty 8. Changes in Latitudes, Changes in Attitudes 9. Boomerang Love 10. Mexico 11. Margaritaville 12. Volcano 13. Fins 14. Southern Cross 15. Growing Older, But Not Up

2004 – License to Chill MAILBOAT/RCA

1. Hey Good Lookin' (with Clint Black, Kenny Chesney, Alan Jackson, Toby Keith & George Strait) 2. Boats to Build (with Alan Jackson) 3. License to Chill (with Kenny Chesney) 4. Coast of Carolina 5. Piece of Work (with Toby Keith) 6. Anything, Anytime, Anywhere 7. Trip Around the Sun (with Martina McBride) 8. Simply Complicated 9. Coastal Confessions 10. Sea of Heartbreak (with George Strait) 11. Conky Tonkin' (with Clint Black) 12. Playin' the Loser Again (with Bill Withers) 13. Window on the World 14. Someone I Used to Love (with Nanci Griffith) 15. Scarlet Begonias 16. Back to the Island

2004 – Live in Hawaii MAILBOAT

DISC 1: Introduction / Don Ho. 1. Great Heart 2. Coconut Telegraph 3. Gypsies in the Palace 4. In The Shelter 5. Burn That Bridge 6. Son of a Son of a Sailor 7. Come Monday 8. The Natives Are Restless Tonight 9. Grapefruit-Juicy Fruit 10. It's Five O' Clock Somewhere 11. One Particular Harbour 12. Cheeseburger in Paradise 13. We Are the People Our Parents Warned Us About 14. Quiet Village (with Martin Denny)

DISC 2: 1. Tiki Bar is Open 2. Everybody's Talkin' 3. Why Don't We Get Drunk (and Screw) 4. Jolly Mon 5. It's My Job 6. Boat Drinks 7. Far Side Of The World 8. A Pirate Looks at Forty 9. Changes in Latitudes, Changes in Attitudes 10. Mexico 11. Margaritaville 12. Volcano (w/Henry Kopono) 13. Fins 14. Back to the Island (new version with Henry Kopono) 15. Stories We Could Tell

BONUS DVD: 1. & 2. General videos 3. Great Heart 4. Why Don't We Get Drunk 5. Volcano (with Henry Kopono) 6. PHans comment 7. Tiny Bubbles (PHan performance)

2004 – A Salty Piece of Land MAILBOAT

1. A Salty Piece of Land (CD single included in the first printing of the novel)

2004 – Selected Shorts - Dan Licks & the Hot Licks SURFDOG

Track 1: Barstool Boogie - Dan Hicks and Jimmy Buffett

2004 – Greatest Hits: Volume II - Alan Jackson ARISTA

Track 17: It's Five O'Clock Somewhere - Alan Jackson and Jimmy Buffett

2004 – Thanks & Giving All Year Long: Marlo Thomas & Friends RHINO/ATLANTIC

Track 5: An Attitude of Gratitude - Jimmy Buffett

2004 – Bridge to Havana CD PYRAMID RECORDS

Track 12: One World - Jimmy Buffett with Mick Fleetwood and Paddy Moloney

2004 – Bridge to Havana DVD PYRAMID RECORDS

Track 2: One World - Jimmy Buffett with Mick Fleetwood and Paddy Moloney

2005 – Down to Earth/High Cumberland Jubilee COLLECTABLES

1. The Christian? 2. Ellis Dee 3. The Missionary 5. A Mile High in Denver 5. The Captain and the Kid 6. Captain America 7. Ain't He A Genius 8. Turnabout 9. There's Nothin' Soft About Hard Times 10. I Can't Be Your Hero Today 11. Truckstop Salvation 12. Ace 13. Rockefeller Square 14. Bend a Little 15. In the Shelter 16. Death Valley Lives 17. Livingston's Gone to Texas 18. England 19. Travelin' Clean 20. The Hangout Gang 21. God Don't Own a Car 22. High Cumberland Jubilee/Comin' Down Slow

2005 – Now Yer Squawkin' RECALL

DISC 1: 1. The Christian? 2. Ellis Dee 3. Richard Frost 4. The Missionary 5. A Mile High in Denver 6. The Captain & the Kid 7. Captain America 8. Ain't He A Genius 9. Turnabout 10. There's Nothing Soft About Hard Times 11. I Can't Be Your Hero Today 12. Truckstop Salvation

DISC 2: 1. Ace 2. Rockefeller Square 3. Bend a Little 4. In the Shelter 5. Death Valley Lives 6. Cumberland High Dilemma 7. Livingston's Gone to Texas 8. England 9. Travelin' Clean 9. The Hangout Gang 10. God Don't Own a Car 11. High Cumberland Jubilee/Comin' Down Slow

2005 – Live at Fenway Park MAILBOAT

DISC 1: 1. Changes in Latitudes, Changes in Attitudes 2. The Great Filling Station Holdup

3. Pencil Thin Mustache 4. Fruitcakes 5. License to Chill 6. Son of a Son of a Sailor 7. Boat Drinks 8. Brown-Eyed Girl 9. Volcano 10. Why Don't We Get Drunk 11. Sweet Caroline 12. Hey Good Lookin' 13. Pascagoula Run 14. One Particular Harbour

DISC 2: 1. Respect 2. Gypsies in the Palace 3. Grapefruit-Juicy Fruit 4. Come Monday 5. Jolly Mon Sing 6. Take Me Out to the Ballgame 7. It's Five O'Clock Somewhere 8. Cheeseburger in Paradise 9. Coast of Carolina 10. Cuban Crime of Passion 11. A Pirate Looks at Forty 12. Piece of Work 13. Margaritaville 14. Fins 15. Scarlet Begonias 16. Southern Cross 17. Defying Gravity

DISC 3 DVD: 1. Fruitcakes 2. License To Chill 3. Son of a Son of a Sailor 4. Boat Drinks 5. Why Don't We Get Drunk 6. Sweet Caroline 7. Respect 8. Jolly Mon Sing 9. Take Me Out to the Ball Game 10. Coast of Carolina 11. Cuban Crime of Passion 12. Southern Cross 13. Defying Gravity

2005 – Hearts in Mind - Nanci Griffith NEW DOOR RECORDS
Track 9. I Love This Town - Nanci Griffith and Jimmy Buffett

2006 – Lotta Love Concert: A Tribute to Nicolette Larson RHINO
Track 14. Margaritaville - Jimmy Buffett

2006 – From the Big Apple to the Big Easy: Madison Sq Garden DVD RHINO/WEA
DISC 2: Track 2. Pascagoula Run 3. Heart of Gold (with Dave Matthews) 4. Son of a Son of a Sailor 5. Fins 6. Margaritaville 7. Sea Cruise (with Paul Simon) 25. When the Saints Go Marching In (with the Neville Brothers, ReBirth Brass Band, Dirty Dozen Brass Band, Dixie Cups, Kermit Ruffins, Dave Bartholomew, Troy Andrews, Ed Bradley)

2006 – *Hoot* Soundtrack MAILBOAT
Track 1. Wondering Where the Lions Are 3. Barefootin' - Jimmy Buffett with Alan Jackson 5. Werewolves of London 7. Floridays 10. Good Guys Win

2006 – Take the Weather With You RCA
1. Bama Breeze 2. Party at the End of the World 3. Weather With You 4. Everybody's on the Phone 5. Whoop De Doo 6. Nothing But A Breeze 7. Cinco de Mayo in Memphis 8. Reggabilly Hill 9. Elvis Presley Blues 10. Hula Girl At Heart 11. Wheel Inside the Wheel 12. Silver Wings 13. Breathe In, Breathe Out, Move On 14. Duke's On Sunday 15. Here We Are (VIDEO TRACK)

2006 – Live at Wrigley Field DVD/CD (same tracks on one disc) MAILBOAT
DISC 1: 1. Piece Of Work 2. Pascagoula Run 3. Hey Good Lookin' 4. Changes in Latitudes 5. I Will Play for Gumbo 6. Come Monday 7. Last Mango in Paris 8. Woman Goin' Crazy On Caroline Street 9. License To Chill 10. Son of a Son of a Sailor 11. Cheeseburger in Paradise 12. Volcano 13. Brown-Eyed Girl

DISC 2: 1. Go Cubs Go 2. Why Don't We Get Drunk 3. La Vie Dansante 4. Banana Republics 5. Southern Cross 6. School Boy Heart 7. A Pirate Looks At Forty 8. Take Me Out to the Ball Game 9. The City 10. It's Five O'Clock Somewhere 11. One Particular Harbour 12. Margaritaville 13. Fins 14. Scarlet Begonias 15. City of New Orleans

2006 – Elton John's Christmas Party HIP-O RECORDS
Track 10. Christmas Island - Jimmy Buffett

2007 – Live at Texas Stadium MCA NASHVILLE
Track 5. All My Ex's Live in Texas - with George Strait 6. Hey Good Lookin' 7. Sea of Heartbreak 8. Northeast Texas Women 9. Boats to Build - with Alan Jackson 10. Margaritaville 11. It's Five O'Clock Somewhere - with Alan Jackson

2007 – *Sports Illustrated* Swimsuit Edition MAILBOAT RECORDS
Track: Getting the Picture (bonus download iTunes)

2007 – Live in Anguilla MAILBOAT
DISC 1: 1. Changes in Latitudes, Changes in Attitudes 2. Domino College 3. Waiting in Vain 4. When Salome Plays the Drum 5. Grapefruit-Juicy Fruit 6. Come Monday 7. They Don't Dance Like Carmen No More 8. It's Five O'Clock Somewhere 9. Cheeseburger in Paradise

10. King of Somewhere Hot 11. Treat Her Like A Lady 12. Still in Paradise 13. Weather With You 14. One Particular Harbour

DISC 2: 1. Brown-Eyed Girl 2. Carnival World 3. Autour Du Rocher 4. Son of a Son of a Sailor 5. That's My Story and I'm Stickin' to It 6. In My Room 7. A Pirate Looks at Forty/Redemption Song 8. Volcano 9. Desperation Samba (Hallowe'en in Tijuana) 10. Margaritaville 11. Southern Cross 12. Fins 13. Distantly in Love 14. Chanson Pour Les Petits Enfants 15.That's What Living is to Me 16. One Particular Harbour

DVD: 1. Chanson Pour Les Petits Enfants 2. That's What Living is to Me 3. One Particular Harbour 4. Domino College 5. When Salome Plays the Drum 6. Cheeseburger in Paradise 7. Treat Her Like A Lady 8. Still in Paradise 9. Changes in Latitudes, Changes in Attitudes 10. Autour Du Rocher 11. It's Five O'Clock Somewhere 12. Son of a Son of a Sailor 13. Volcano 14. Desperation Samba 15. Margaritaville 16. A Pirate Looks at Forty 17. Fins 18. Distantly in Love

2008 – From the Reach - Sonny Landreth LANDFALL
Track 6. Howlin' Moon - Sonny Landreth and Jimmy Buffett

2008 – Join the Band - Little Feat 429 RECORDS
Track 5. Champion of the World - Little Feat and Jimmy Buffett 8. Time Loves A Hero - Little Feat and Jimmy Buffett

2008 – Nod to the Storyteller - Nadirah Shakoor MAILBOAT
Track 10. Son of a Son of a Sailor - with Jimmy Buffett 11. Volcano 12. When This War is Over - with Jimmy Buffett

2009 – Scenes You Know by Heart DVD MAILBOAT
1. Cheeseburger in Paradise 2. He Went to Paris 3. Fins 4. Son of a Son of a Sailor 5. A Pirate Looks at Forty 6. Margaritaville 7. Come Monday 8. Changes in Latitudes, Changes in Attitudes 9. Why Don't We Get Drunk 10. Pencil Thin Moustache 11. Grapefruit-Juicy Fruit 12. Boat Drinks 13. Volcano 14. Hey Good Lookin' 15. It's Five O'Clock Somewhere

2009 – Buffet Hotel MAILBOAT
1. Nobody from Nowhere 2. Wings 3. Big Top 4. Beautiful Swimmers 5. Turn Up the Heat and Chill the Rose 6. Summerzcool 7. Rhumba Man 8. We Learned to be Cool from You 9. Surfing in a Hurricane 10. Life Short, Call Now 11. Buffet Hotel 12. A Lot to Drink About

2010 – Encores MAILBOAT
DISC 1: 1. Come Monday 2. Tin Cup Chalice 3. Growing Older But Not Up 4. Coast of Carolina 5. Paradise 6. Do You Know What It Means to Miss New Orleans 7. Nautical Wheelers 8. Trying to Reason with Hurricane Season 9. Banana Republics 10. He Went to Paris 11. Last Mango in Paris

DISC 2: 1. L'air De La Louisiane 2. Reggabilly Hill 3. Coast of Marseilles 4. Lovely Cruise 5. Oysters And Pearls 6. Wildflowers 7. Defying Gravity 8. It's A Big Old Goofy World 9. Death of An Unpopular Poet 10. Blowin' in the Wind 11. A Pirate Looks At Forty

2010 – Margaritaville (live) - Jimmy Buffett and Bret Michaels MAILBOAT
Digital download single

2010 – 34 Number Ones - Alan Jackson SONY NASHVILLE/ARISTA
Track 33. It's Five O'Clock Somewhere - Alan Jackson and Jimmy Buffett

2010 – You Get What You Give - Zac Brown Band ATLANTIC
Track 2. Knee Deep - Zac Brown Band and Jimmy Buffett

2010 – Coral Reefer Christmas - Robert Greenidge MAILBOAT
Track 3. Winter Wonderland - Coral Reefer Band with Jimmy Buffett vocal

2012 – Tuskegee - Lionel Richie MERCURY NASHVILLE
Track 13. All Night Long - Lionel Richie and Jimmy Buffett with the Coral Reefer Band

2012 – Welcome to Fin City DVD/CD MAILBOAT
Disc: 1 DVD 1. Viva Las Vegas 2. Brown Eyed Girl 3. License to Chill 4. Pencil Thin Mustache

5. Off to See the Lizard 6. Life is Just a Tire Swing 7. Bama Breeze 8. Gypsies in the Palace 9. It's Midnight and I'm Not Famous Yet 10. Grapefruit-Juicy Fruit 11. School Boy Heart 12. Changes in Latitudes, Changes in Attitudes 13. One Particular Harbour 14. Fins

Disc: 2 CD 1. Viva Las Vegas 2. Brown Eyed Girl 3. License to Chill 4. Off to See the Lizard 5. Life is Just a Tire Swing 6. Bama Breeze 7. Gypsies in the Palace 8. It's Midnight and I'm Not Famous Yet 9. Knee Deep 10. Back Where I Come From 11. Changes in Latitudes, Changes in Attitudes 12. One Particular Harbour 13. Fins 14. Defying Gravity 15. Elvis Presley Blues

2013 – Songs From St. Somewhere MAILBOAT

1. Somethin' 'Bout A Boat 2. Einstein Was A Surfer 3. Earl's Dead - Cadillac For Sale 4. Too Drunk to Karaoke 5. Serpentine 6. Useless But Important Information 7. I Want to Go Back to Cartagena 8. Soulfully 9. Rue de La Guitare 10. I'm No Russian 11. Tides 12. The Rocket That Grandpa Rode 13. I Wave Bye Bye 14/ Colour of the Sun 15. Oldest Surfer on the Beach 16. I Want to Go Back to Cartagena (Spanish version)

2014 Cheesecakes – Live at Alpine Valley video download /digital single MAILBOAT

2015 Strangers Again – Judy Collins WILDFLOWER/CLEOPATRA RECORDS

Track 9. Someday Soon - Judy Collins with Jimmy Buffett

2105 35 MPH Town – Toby Keith SHOW DOG UNIVERSAL MUSIC

Track 8. Sailboat for Sale - Toby Keith with Jimmy Buffett

2015 Ever Elusive Future - MAILBOAT **digital single**

2015 Workin' N Playin' - MAILBOAT **digital single**

2016 – 'Tis the SeaSon MAILBOAT

1. Wonderful Christmastime 2. Jingle Bell Rock 3. All I Want for Christmas is My Two Front Teeth 4. Drivin' the Pig (Manejando el Cerdo) 5. The Twelve Days of Christmas (Parrothead Version) 6. What I Didn't Get for Christmas 7. Rockin' Around the Christmas Tree 8. Rudolph the Red-Nosed Reindeer 9. Santa Stole Thanksgiving 10. Mele Kalikimaka (feat. Jake Shimabukuro) 11. Winter Wonderland (feat. Robert Greenidge) 12. Baby, It's Cold Outside (feat. Nadirah Shakoor) 13. White Christmas

About the Author & the Photographer

OLAF NORDSTROM is a bartender/writer/fisherman/carpenter/philosopher/ sailor/raconteur of little repute who hails originally from the sands of Cape Cod.

After forsaking nearly everything which was his (including his own name), he set up life aboard his sailboat, SV Honky's Dory, then took a bearing south by southwest to gunkhole among the Elizabeth Islands. Much of what little time he spends ashore each summer is usually around the docks and bars of Woods Hole on the Cape, as well as those on Nantucket and the Vineyard. Not one to drop his anchor for long, though, Nordstrom eventually sets course in the late autumn to head even further south to Crab Key, where he spends the season cooking, eating, drinking, fishing, sailing, reading, writing, playing his saxophone, and spending as little time working as the rest of the world will allow. Needless to say, Nordstrom loves the now.

Since sometime in the early 1970s, Nordstrom has been holder of the Guinness Book of World Records, as well as the writer of The Essential Book of Boat Drinks & Assorted Frozen Concoctions, The Margaritaville Cookbook, and Jimmy's Buffet: Food for Feeding Friends & Feeding Frenzies. He is still working on The Essential Book of Tequila. Not long ago, Honky's Dory settled on the bottom, and Nordstrom is now the master of a newer vessel, Victorious Egret.

JIM SHEA, whose photography graces the covers of Jimmy's earliest albums, has shared an outtake from the Songs You Know by Heart photo shoot for this cover.

Whether on a soundstage directing Faith Hill, or on some exotic South Sea island shooting Jimmy Buffett, Jim creates memorable images in any setting. Born in Manhattan, he trained on Madison Avenue in the world of advertising photography before heading to LA and into the entertainment industry. Aerosmith, Bonnie Raitt, Fleetwood Mac, Linda Ronstadt, Elton John, and the Eagles were but a few of the subjects of his award-winning images on album covers and posters, as well as in Rolling Stone.

Not long after, record labels recruited Jim to direct music videos, and his innovative approach established him as a creative pioneer. In recent years, he has received numerous awards and nominations from the National Academy of Recording Arts and Sciences, the Country Music Association, and the Academy of Country Music.

A lot more of Jim's work with Jimmy, as well as with others, can be found at:

WWW.JIMSHEAPHOTOGRAPHY.COM

Made in United States
North Haven, CT
06 December 2024

61880099R00137